Leading Primary Care

This new book of leadership narratives portrays the reality of driving change within primary care, making it a valuable resource for a broad primary care audience. It empowers both clinicians and non-clinicians by helping them recognise and harness their leadership qualities. The book weaves together stories from diverse primary care practitioners operating at various levels, from junior to senior, in both clinical practice and large-scale operations. These narratives showcase how these professionals applied their leadership skills, navigated challenges, and distilled valuable lessons from their experiences.

To enhance the reader's understanding, the editors have added their own insights to each contribution, emphasising the lessons that the broader community can glean. Rather than reiterating theoretical concepts, they refer back to their companion book, *The Leadership Hike.*

Whether read independently or alongside *The Leadership Hike*, this book serves as an invaluable reference for all team members, regardless of clinical background. It is especially pertinent for GP trainees and trainers, given the incorporation of leadership and quality improvement into the licensing qualification for general practice (MRCGP).

Leading Primary Care

Tales from the Leadership Hikers

Edited by
Amar Rughani and Joanna Bircher

CRC Press
Taylor & Francis Group
Boca Raton London New York

CRC Press is an imprint of the
Taylor & Francis Group, an **informa** business

First edition published 2024
by CRC Press
2385 NW Executive Center Drive, Suite 320, Boca Raton, FL 33431

and by CRC Press
4 Park Square, Milton Park, Abingdon, Oxon, OX14 4RN

CRC Press is an imprint of Taylor & Francis Group, LLC

ISBN: 978-1-032-21901-1 (hbk)
ISBN: 978-1-032-21899-1 (pbk)
ISBN: 978-1-003-27049-2 (ebk)

DOI: 10.1201/9781003270492

Typeset in Bembo
by Apex CoVantage, LLC]

Contents

Podcasts to accompany the book can be found here:
https://elearning.rcgp.org.uk/mod/page/view.php?id=13316

These have been created with the support of RCGP Learning and are available to all.

Foreword

Modern healthcare is rapidly changing and evolving; it has high challenge, high risk, and high rewards, and thus requires excellent leadership at all levels to ensure patient care is optimised and health and care professionals are supported and nurtured. Consequently, much has been written about leadership and medicine, indeed it seems to be a magnet for authors and opinion makers.

What makes this book, and indeed the wider approach to the subject, so refreshing is that it is authentically different. By building on the original book *The Leadership Hike: Shaping Primary Care Together*, Amar Rughani and Joanna Bircher have turned a great book into a dynamic, creative, and very versatile suite of resources – the approach of interviewing and collating the views of a diverse range of leaders and then drawing out the subject matter, turning it into a set of personal questions and challenges is really effective. The accompanying podcasts are there for readers to turn to, to listen in selectively, and to pick and choose the people that had piqued their curiosity and hear it in the authentic voice – for those that love podcasts, of course every interview is of great value. This flexible approach is energising and allows people to absorb, reflect and utilise this work in whatever way works best for them.

As I worked through the 14 cases I was struck by the vast array of paths and experiences these medical leaders have had, and their differing approaches and strategies for leading. However, some themes can be readily established – humility is almost universal, commitment is clearly evident, and passion for the cause is a golden thread – be it a narrow focus or a great big ambition.

To quote Sheinaz Stansfield:

> Training and titles do not make leaders. To me, leadership is a way of being and connecting with people. It is about inspiring, supporting, nurturing, and empowering others – holding their hand as they become the best possible versions of themselves. Leaders have empathy and a desire to improve things. Then listen to and rally with their people, together moving toward a shared purpose.

Primary healthcare professionals have a remarkable array of talents and experiences from which to draw, and countless opportunities to apply new knowledge. However, what we are all short of is the time to invest in our personal development and the resources to dedicate to being our best selves. Having had a long and varied medical career that has included many positions of visible and less visible leadership, I have had time to research and learn what others think about it, as well as forming a few opinions of my own! I am truly delighted to be recommending this book and suite of resources to you – I trust that you will find them as inspiring and thought-provoking as I have done, and that in turn you will pay it forward, by sharing these with your friends and colleagues so that we can all benefit from the practical wisdom herein.

Prof Dame Helen Stokes-Lampard
DBE PhD FRCGP FLSW
Chair of the Academy of Medical Royal Colleges

Preface

Why do we care about leadership? Because we've seen how good leadership liberates people, freeing them to contribute strongly when they are given the opportunity to grow and the support to succeed. The belief that much more of this is needed led us to write *The Leadership Hike*, giving our perspective on effective leadership in primary care. The feedback we had was very encouraging; readers appreciated the ideas and the information, and in particular they liked the examples illustrating how leadership is applied in real life.

This companion volume takes that process of bringing leadership to life a stage further. We believe that leadership cannot be taught, but it can be learned through life experience. For this book, we were very fortunate to obtain reflections on the lives of 14 leaders. Each of them thought deeply and shared something of the difficult lessons they learned, in the hope that this would help others. We are profoundly grateful to them not only for contributing, but for being open about themselves and in particular, their vulnerabilities.

Effective leadership is not the right of the few. It can come from anywhere and this is reflected in the range of our contributors. They come from different roles in the team from GPs to managers, from different levels of experience, influence, and responsibility and from different parts of the world.

Because we feel strongly about leadership (strongly enough to write a book), we recognise that we can't help but be biased about the nature of effective leadership. This book challenges our viewpoint, helping readers to gain a deeper insight by illustrating leadership through many perspectives beyond our own.

Which leads us to a caveat and a request. Just because something is written in black and white, it is important not to grant it too much authority. The opinions in this book are not statements of fact, and the questions that we ask in the text may encourage you to think in certain ways. So, stand back and take a balcony view, survey the experience of others, ask your own questions, and discover yourselves more deeply.

Books can sometimes be greater than the sum of their parts. We hope that the cumulative effect of these stories is that they inspire you to become the leader you hope to be.

Amar Rughani and Joanna Bircher

Editors

Dr Amar Rughani MBE FRCGP

Amar Rughani was a GP in Chapelgreen Practice Sheffield for over 30 years, with a number of senior roles in GP education, examining and curriculum development. He was Provost of the RCGP in South Yorkshire and North Trent, during which time he encouraged inclusiveness and diversity in the team. Amar and Joanna are passionate about giving people the confidence and opportunity to make a difference in their communities. This led to their first joint publication, *The Leadership Hike*, and Amar continues to work to develop leadership, especially amongst younger practitioners from across the primary care team.

Dr Joanna Bircher MB ChB FRCGP

Joanna Bircher is a GP in Greater Manchester. She is Clinical Director of Greater Manchester GP Excellence Programme, a Generation Q Fellow of the Health Foundation, and an RCGP Clinical Adviser. She has a master's degree in leadership for quality improvement from Ashridge Business School and is co-author of the *RCGP Guide to Quality Improvement*. Her particular interest is in making established QI methodology relevant and accessible for primary care and encouraging all who work within healthcare to develop their leadership skills. In 2020 she co-authored *The Leadership Hike: Shaping Primary Care Together* (CRC Press).

Introduction: The Leadership Resources

As a broad statement, we feel that leadership is more an art than a science and lends itself to being learned through experience rather than to being taught.

To assist that process, we have developed three resources that we hope will guide you.

The first is the book *The Leadership Hike*, which describes many of the features of effective compassionate leadership and uses examples to illustrate the concepts. The book has the shape of a journey but is a description of leadership rather than leaders.

Because leadership is principally about people, the second book, *Leading Primary Care – Tales from the Leadership Hikers*, is a book of life stories. It complements the original book by relating the experience and insights of people who find themselves, often unexpectedly, taking a lead role in an area they care about.

The majority of the contributors have also been in discussion with us, reflecting on their experiences in a series of podcasts, which connect us more strongly with their stories and add further depth. These podcasts are the third element of the leadership resource and can be accessed by QR code at the end of each relevant chapter.

Whichever of the three resources you come to first, the other two will help you on your own journey of discovery. Between them, they shine a light from different perspectives and allow you to understand leadership more deeply and just as importantly, because this is where good leadership starts, to also understand yourself better.

We hope very much that you enjoy them and find them helpful.

Dr Amar Rughani
Dr Joanna Bircher

SECTION

1

Tales from the Leadership Hikers

CHAPTER

1

Ollie Hart

Dr Ollie Hart's background is as a GP partner in a large inner-city practice in Sheffield and as clinical director for a primary care network, working alongside other local leaders to improve services. As a doctor and an individual, he wishes to support the health and social systems that help people develop their capabilities, enabling them to maximise the achievements they value and the opportunities their lives offer. This passion has led him to develop an enterprise that teaches and supports coaching.

I've tried to think of my top five tips for surviving and thriving in a leadership role. I don't think many leaders set out to be in the position they find themselves in. Often, I think leadership finds you, selecting out people prepared to put themselves on the line and give it a go. Of course, when the opportunity finds you, it can lead to a relentless oscillation between do I or don't I? Am I good enough or not? Is it worth it? I think this questioning is normal of leadership for most people.

My tips are offered to help you enjoy the ride and push you towards believing in yourself. In my opinion, without self-belief and a sense of satisfaction in what you pursue, leadership is a toil destined to wither. There's no shame in that, leading is definitely not for everyone, and not all the time for any of us. But I think if you find yourself there and you are brave enough to give it your best shot, it can expand your horizons and enrich your experience of life.

DOI: 10.1201/ 9781003270492-2

1. Seeking purpose and agency, together

Have you ever had the experience of pursuing something that holds deep meaning for you? When your sense of purpose was so strong that it gave you energy, a seemingly inexhaustible source of fuel and enthusiasm? Those long hours flew by, the effort, sacrifice, and commitment felt like a privilege, a mission, not a job.

This is the first tip I want to share with you. I think generally I've seen most success for anyone, be they patients, leaders, or those seeking to perform well, if they can connect with something that holds a deep meaning for them.

It can be challenging enough for many to decide what matters most, it may take quite a journey to decide. It's often not a linear decision-making process. Our views change, but good leaders keep that ongoing process bubbling away in the background, checking in and refining, but making sure it still feels right. Some of this may be judged by the 'logic of the head', but often it is the 'passion of the heart'. Maybe you are checking in with others you trust, and at times you may decide to modify your ambitions to fit the needs of others. But ultimately if you are pulled too far from what really matters to you, you are likely to lose energy and motivation.

But there is more. You need to ensure you are capable of pursuing what matters most in a meaningful way. This means being in control of the pursuit of your prize. Control is not necessarily about finding it easy or simple, the boldest goals usually are not, but it is about being the director of your own journey. It can be bravely ambitious, but the prime determinant of success needs to sit primarily with you.

To help with this, seek out fellow journeyers. In my experience journeying alone is no fun; a shared purpose is so much more satisfying. It can be more complicated than solo work; it involves negotiation, sharing vulnerabilities and doubts and failures. But it allows you to celebrate success together. Seeking your shared purpose, ensuring it is within your collective control as a team, and working on it together is the formula for a rewarding leadership journey, in my opinion.

I think I learnt most about this when developing our training company Peak Health Coaching. I started it with a GP colleague. We got to know each other when we were working as GPs with an interest in pain management. We both chose this area as we recognised the burden of distress associated with living with chronic pain. A life lived with enduring constant pain can be absolutely miserable. As a doctor, the sense of helplessness in not being able to offer a meaningful cure has a big impact. However, we realised the secret of success most often lay in people retaking control and resetting the parameters of how their nervous system functioned. Not easy, and often involving a mixture of biological, psychological, and social factors. However, it cemented the value of coaching approaches for us both. The more we looked, the more we recognised the value of this approach in the most complex and distressing conditions we faced as GPs.

As two different people, we didn't always view things the same and recognised that each of us prioritised some aspects of coaching more than others. We made time to hear each other out, understand, but not always completely agree. However, we both recognised that the skills to work in this way were severely hampered by a lack of good training. Our shared purpose was forged.

We believed we could improve the lives of people who really needed a different approach, by training our colleagues to think and work in a different way. The subsequent hours, many late at night and over weekends, have been fuelled by that passion. We are comfortable to challenge each other and to disagree, recognising that there is rarely one-size-fits-all for anything, and to maintain a range of options for teaching and implementing.

Given the number of mistakes we've made, we've needed that fuel. We've drawn confidence to experiment, challenge each other, and review and revise, supported by our sense that what we are doing is worth the effort. It does require ongoing optimism and hope, but you can deliberately work on that. I think the fact that we are trying something ambitious and interesting continues the shared adventure. If you get it right, the pursuit of this shared purpose becomes tangibly exciting.

In a lot of ways, we continue to 'seek' our shared purpose, because there is a sense this is a never-ending journey. You could find this dispiriting, losing motivation. I think it helps to come to terms with leadership as involving a 'perpetual pursuit' rather than needing to arrive at a specific destination. You can get to the top of a mountain, but you can usually see another in the distance waiting to be climbed. The higher you climb, the more you see! This takes us on to point 2.

2. Keeping going, finding ways to enjoy the grind

Amar and Joanna highlight the essential leadership skill of 'digging deep'. It's certainly been part of my learning journey to realise the importance of resilience and persistence. I've observed that often this is driven by fear of failure or anxiety about being made to look bad. I think it works much better and is far more sustainable if you can find an angle that you enjoy. It's exhausting to maintain persistent effort driven by negative emotions, but it's recharging and sustainable to be driven by positive emotions.

If you can find a way to love the 'training' as much as the 'outcomes', you'll always keep positive.

Of course, often it is a mix of both positive and negative. I remember changing schools at the age of 10. At that time football was my life, and I was petrified that I would arrive at the new, bigger school as one of the worst players and be left out of the teams. Over the summer holidays I practiced every day. I invented imaginary games up and down the garden. I was Bryan Robson crossing for Kevin Keegan to score (sorry, that shows my age!). It was end-to-end stuff, FA cup finals, European Championships, and World Cups! I became so absorbed in the make-believe, the practice was happening by itself. Refining my shots into the bottom corner, for the winning goal in front of a make-believe Wembley crowd, overshadowed the initial fear-based motivation.

As it turned out, all the dribbling on my own paid off. To my pleasant surprise I arrived at my new school to discover I was one of the better players. Certainly not the best, but enough to build confidence. This sort of approach builds its own internal momentum, as you start to trust that even if you're not the best, or even at a beginner stage, you can enjoy a supportive internal dialogue. 'Keep plugging away and it will work out in the end. . . . Even if you don't "succeed" now, you'll have gained from the experience'. Once you see some return on your trying, it encourages you to keep going.

Whether it was that summer of solo football practice or subsequent progress through sustained efforts, I've been fortunate enough to retain that positive inner dialogue. That positive internal narrative, encouraging and reassuring, has been one of my most useful assets. I hear many people talk of persecutory inner voices, but mine tends to reassure me that 'it will be alright', 'You're giving things your best shot'. It's not completely unshakeable and needs nurturing, but I'm mindful of its value. As I've grown to realise that value, I tend to try to notice what I could suggest that would be both encouraging and forgiving. I'm not necessarily advocating talking out loud to yourself and I'll reassure you that I don't hear real voices, but I do practise taking a little time to purposefully consider what I could tell myself that would be supportive and useful.

I think it helps to prepare yourself for a sustained effort in whatever leadership role you take on. What do you need to focus on? How can you 'gamify' or reframe things for yourself to make the daily grind enjoyable, like I did with the football practice in the garden? Meaningful change is likely to take time, so a few games along the way help it to feel less of a grind.

As a final aside, I've always been a fan of staying physically fit. In my experience, when you are physically fit and take time to regularly tap into those exercise endorphins, you tend to have more energy for life. You've probably realised by now, I'm someone who likes to squeeze as much value as I can out of the limited time we have alive. For me, being fit generates more zest for life, which give more fuel for what I'm thinking or doing, which tends to reap rewards in terms of success and good feedback. It's a self-perpetuating cycle of having enough energy, reward, and encouragement.

As with everything, make sure the exercise is a positive experience for you. If it's a drag, and something you feel you 'have to do' rather than something you 'want to do', it is very hard to maintain, and can lower your energy levels. Whether it's doing it with a friend, as part of a team, or picking an activity that really interests you or gives you a new skill to learn, try to work to find exercise you enjoy. True, you can learn to love the endorphins, but I'd recommend some effort finding something you love in the first place.

3. Keeping your thinking (and energy) in perspective

People often find themselves in leadership positions because they think they have a great way of doing something. Even if they don't necessarily have the best idea, they often feel the need to force through their ideas to maintain their status as 'The Boss'. In my experience, not only is this exhausting (How can you come up with all the best ideas all the time?); it is not very effective.

I've mentioned already that I've discovered the value of coaching techniques to support people with complex health issues. Seeing the success of how people respond to this in a health setting has encouraged me to transfer these ways of thinking and doing to other parts of life.

One of the most valuable insights I've gathered from health coaching is this 'release' from being the problem-solver. Generally, people do much better working with ideas and approaches that they develop themselves, with the right support and information of course. Their thinking is forged from their bank of day-to-day experiences and their context. This is the very same context in which they will need to enact any changes or development. No matter how brilliant a coach you are, you'll not know what that life is really like. You can never understand their day-to-day feelings and experiences as they perceive them.

I think it is the same as a leader working with a team. Following a leader's ideas and plan is far less inspiring and motivating than being supported to pursue your own. Leaders can't ever fully appreciate the context of their team.

But there is a catch here. What if your team is not as motivated and driven as you? You may find yourself leading because you passionately believe in something. You'll probably have thought a lot about the subject matter, read around the topic, and talked it over. Your job description, bonus scheme, or potential for reputational gain may also be driving you harder than others around you.

There is a tough balance to find here. You want to inject your enthusiasm and energy, inspire, and of course develop hard-thought-out ideas. However, the risk is always that the more brilliant you are, the less others are able to shine. Too much of your thinking, no matter how well intentioned, can smother others. There is a skill in fuelling your own burning ambition without scorching others close to you.

I've drawn inspiration here from Barack Obama. His second book, *The Audacity of Hope*, refers to a boldness and bravery of pushing through what you think matters and is important. He certainly had to draw on much 'audacity' to bring Obamacare into reality. I think this translates into the 'audacity of leadership'. I think you need to be conscious of balancing your own ego and belief that your ideas are worth pursuing and driving, but leaving room for alternative perspectives and for other people's egos to flourish too. If you know you can be an overbearing personality, ensuring others have express permission to challenge you and a safe opportunity to do so is an important balancing factor. It can be worth taking a moment to reflect, 'What's it like to be on the receiving end of me?'

I've personally experienced this working closely with a manager who had quite different views and ideas to mine as a clinical lead. It was tempting to use my status as a clinician and owner in the business to 'outrank' him and force my perspective to the fore. Sometimes out of frustration or impatience, I would do this. But for every step forward I thought we were making, this approach pushed our progress two steps back. I learnt when key members of your team feel unfairly overruled, they find ways to undermine you and they dig resistance into the system. Everyone has relationships and spheres of influence, and I found that the disharmony I had created played out in that manager exerting undue influence in the areas they did have control and dominance over, to subtly stall or undermine the progress I wanted to make. I think it was often not even deliberate, but played out in a subconscious defence of their ego and status.

In the end, it is what people do when they are not with you that matters more than how they talk or act when you are around. It might seem satisfying to have people agree with your ideas in meetings, but it really doesn't work if they disagree with them outside meetings because they feel their ideas and thoughts have been neglected.

I think your key job as a leader is to ensure that the shared purpose you hold as a group is well understood, manageable, and most importantly matters to your team. If the goal you pursue is considered important enough, if people believe it's worth it, they will work hard to come up with ideas and solutions that work for them and those around them. I think it is the most satisfying aspect of leadership to recognise when the ideas and efforts of your team have achieved the success you all pursue.

4. Making peace with time

How often do we find ourselves feeling we just don't have enough time to do all the things we want to do, whether it is a long list of things we want to accomplish or experience, or an area that needs more attention? Often, we know that more time thinking and planning around an issue will lead to better quality outcomes; we want time to go deeper.

This can feel like a real pressure, a burden that we carry physically and psychologically. It tightens our shoulders, and we feel it as a constricting band around our head. Sometimes it sits as a barely contained sense of panic, waiting to explode. Sometimes it does, and we are overwhelmed and sleepless with the volume of stuff we must do.

One of the most helpful shifts in perspective I think I've learnt is to value the time I *do* spend on things, rather than focus on the time I'm not spending on others. It is still a work in progress, but regaining a sense of control of how you choose to spend your time is a liberating freedom.

No one, not even the most capable and confident people, can make more time. Perhaps you can become more efficient and quicker at jobs, but there is a limit, and going faster can mean you are cutting corners. It is good to know this. It helps you to value where you spend your time and to choose wisely.

When you are working alone, consider what matters most to you. What are your priorities. What are the things that mean the most to you? Make sure your time is focused on that. That might take a little planning and honest soul-searching, but it pays dividends in the end.

When you are working with others, negotiate the best use of your shared time. Whether it is a one-to-one consultation or a group meeting, some time spent planning your shared priorities and where to spend your time is important. I often find my opening line as a GP is, 'What should we talk about to get best value out of our 10 minutes together?' If it is clear that you need more time on a particular topic, you can always negotiate for a follow-up, or shift priority away from other items. But a shared appreciation of the time available is respectful to all parties.

For me working as a GP, it transformed my perception of the 10-minute consultation. Instead of seeing time as a 'tormentor', criticising me for not squeezing in everything I thought I ought to do, I started to see it as a 10-minute 'opportunity'. The time is set and known to both of us; the challenge is to use that time to achieve some kind of positive change –ideally, a change that the patient determined, recognising what was possible.

(As an aside, I've started to appreciate the times in my 10-minute consultations when the patient is thinking – you know, looking off into space and really thinking – as being the 'golden moments'. The more of these I can provoke in our 10 minutes, the better I judge it has gone. It's my key marker of success).

There is a range of useful techniques around making the most of your time in meetings; preparation and realistic agendas with clear articulation of the aim of your shared time all help. They often form the baseline of quality improvement courses, worth exploring a version that chimes for you.

The bottom line is to free yourself from the stress of time limits. You will make much better use of the time you do have, and value what you do spend time on, rather than regret what you didn't. Make peace with time; make it your friend.

5. Doing it the right way, not the fast way

This last tip probably pulls them all together.

When working on anything we feel strongly about, we are often impatient to see results fast. We search for markers of success to validate our leadership role. It can be tempting to want to employ tactics to get the outcome as quickly as we can. If you are a parent, this might mean just quickly doing up the shoelaces of your child, so you can get out the house quickly. How often as a parent with small children are you running late for the next activity? In the health context, it plays out as using quick-fix medication rather than the more involved and complex option of supporting lifestyle change. How often do we decide as a GP in a 10-minute consultation that it's simpler to prescribe than to explain and encourage lifestyle changes? Often GP income is conditional on patients hitting targets, and we've learnt the fastest way to achieve those targets is to cajole people into adding another tablet to their daily regime.

In the leadership context, it is often tempting to simply make a plan and tell people what we are doing. It can seem like the fastest way of achieving results: just follow my instructions. But in my experience, tempting as this is, it just doesn't get the results you want in the end.

The child that never gets the chance to tie their laces always relies on their parent to make the time to do it. A diabetic patient that accumulates more medications usually puts on weight and becomes even more disempowered in their self-management capabilities. This inevitably leads to worse outcomes. A team member who doesn't have the chance to contribute to the mission, shared purpose, and methods for achieving them in the end disengages or, worse, disrupts.

Ultimately, in my view, leadership is usually a long game; it takes persistence and patience. For many significant leadership roles, often you don't necessarily expect to be there at the 'finish'. In this complex world of wicked problems, you are merely the guardian of the 'leadership baton', seeking to run your leg as best you can and pass on to the next enthusiast.

If you appreciate that most meaningful change takes time, it can focus your attention on how you are doing things in the now, rather than always looking off to the future.

You can ensure people are involved, relationships are being nurtured, and a range of ideas are considered. It can be sensible to design checkpoints and opportunities to celebrate achievements, but I would recommend as many of these being about *how* you are working as about the outcomes you have achieved.

So those are my top five tips right now. The trouble with writing anything down is that it is not long before your thinking has developed. New conversations, new experiences, and learnings have nudged you in a slightly different direction. I hope my thoughts will do exactly that for you, give you some food for thought, maybe an idea to discuss with someone or mull over on a walk or in the bath. They will only ever be a gentle provocation to the thoughts you hold. It's important to reflect, but also to try things out. I hope you can bravely maintain that balance as you give leadership a go!

Commentary

Ollie burns brightly. At some point in our lives, we may also hope to feel the power of passion and its ability to energise us to do tough and courageous things. Ollie is aware of this energy and how it can manifest itself both as useful propulsion and sometimes as harmful heat.

Ollie's energy comes from being engaged in work that has meaning for him, and he reminds us that in our lives, our relationship with time is important. How we use that time to do fulfilling work and how we make peace with time so that we are not overly restricted by it, is what we will now explore.

How important is doing meaningful work to you? Have you compromised on other rewards such as pay or status, to do work that matters to you? If not, should you?

Effective leaders have strong drive, and this can tempt them to believe that others in the team feel driven too, maybe to similar degrees. As always, the reality is that we are all different. What drives different people will vary and may not be as strong or as aligned with what leaders feel is the team's purpose. Sometimes the drive that people have may not be related to work at all. The question is, does any of that matter?

Do you know what principally drives your colleagues, particularly key individuals? How do you feel if they don't care about things in the way that you do? How does this make you behave towards them?

Having a purpose – sometimes called a 'Why' – is widely promoted in the leadership literature because it describes a connection with a deep source of energy that both drives and sustains us. That's important, but the notion of 'purpose' is for many people abstract and difficult to articulate. It may feel alienating to be asked to say what our motivation is, and there's also the fear that we may say the wrong thing, maybe something that isn't acceptable. Have you ever had that experience? It can be a particular issue in organisations that have a very strong set of values and assumed purpose. The NHS is a good example of this.

If we look deeper, though, if we assume that colleagues want to do a good job and help people, we can be more relaxed about what they are energised by and whether their 'Why' resonates with our own.

Nevertheless, we still want to connect people to *their* drives because that connection fuels them. This involves helping others to be aware of their drives and not be anxious if these don't mirror what drives their leaders. However, to encourage people in this way, as Ollie does, takes humility and generosity, which is why it is rare.

For many people, coming to work may be driven by the need to earn rather than anything grander. That doesn't mean they don't have helpful values or the capacity to devote themselves; indeed, validating them for what they *are* can boost motivation.

In what ways do you make people feel validated for the work that they do? If they come principally to earn a wage, do you recognise or encourage that?

Doing a good job, even without a self-declared passion, is a great purpose in itself, but there is another dimension. As people grow in knowledge, skills, and attitudes, more opportunities open up and with these, more experiences through which to find greater meaning in the workplace. We see this with people who are junior and may be new to the practice. As they learn the ropes they do better work, start feeling valued, and seek increasingly meaningful goals. In this way, purpose may grow with capability.

Taking this further, there are a couple of things that might make us more effective leaders. First, we could take the (often implied) pressure off our colleagues to sign up to the 'Right Why'. For example, we may become more aware of our passion and learn not to 'scorch' others by overpersuading them or showing approval of the motivation of some but not of others. Leadership is more the art of connecting with people than converting them, and there is no right *why*, just as there is no right *way*.

Second, we may take active steps to find out what drives others, starting with the simple but powerful act of asking and listening to what they are interested in. We can notice what gives them joy and recognise when they are flagging because they are losing connection with what's important to them. In fact, not doing these things is not a neutral act. Once we sense what matters to them, we can fan their flames, not just ours.

Ollie illustrates his 'growth mindset' not just in wanting to improve through learning, but in wanting others to grow too. We can nurture the confidence and self-esteem of others partly by not allowing our own drives, needs, and methods to dominate. The last of these is interesting, and Ollie touches on the importance of letting people do things their own way even when we have the knowledge, experience, and authority to insist on our methods.

People who see and do things differently from us are often felt as difficult. A good leader will not only give permission to do things differently but will not sabotage, which is often done subtly, and will find a way to congratulate success. Such a leader might say, 'Well done. I wouldn't have done it that way, but I'd have been wrong, and you've shown it can work'. Such a leader would also not punish failure but seek to learn from it.

Who in your team do you find difficult? How could you help them to rise in self-esteem and even in reputation? Why might you avoid claiming some of the credit as your own?

We also help others to grow by reducing the 'noise', or in other words, those things that distract people and make it hard for them to feel motivated.

What is the noise in your workplace that causes demotivation and could be addressed? Patient complaints and anger, pointless tick-boxing, irritating admin, and lack of kindness are some examples, but what are yours? What action could you take to reduce the noise?

So far, we've described how we use our time to be meaningfully employed through being connected to what buzzes us, but Ollie also reflects on how time pressure can restrict, control, and feel like it's against us. We can't change time. Possibly, we could use time more efficiently. However, we *can* change our relationship with time by shifting our attitude.

In life, the journey of discovery and learning is often more significant than any endpoints, and 'time' is the medium through which that journey happens. Taking time allows us to appreciate important things that we don't if our lives are too dense with information and too controlled by expectations. Giving ourselves the space to notice and for reflection to give birth to insight is not a trivial matter. These insights lead to appreciation both of life and of people and are the 'golden moments' that Ollie describes.

Creating space does not remain optional for those who have been brave enough to try to use time differently. We say 'brave' because it is tough to make different choices for how we use our time in an NHS culture which insists that we prioritise targets and deadlines. Not all of these actually matter, even if they are evidence-based.

Have you ever deprioritised a target? How do you currently build space into your crowded life? Who could support you to do this?

Enlightened leaders can help shift attitudes and priorities so that time, the most precious commodity of all, is used better. Time well spent helps us to appreciate life, to allow deeper lessons to be learned at their own pace and ensure that the joy of living is not squandered by rushing on to the next target.

Ollie is a champion for living purposeful lives. A life with meaning is always possible, but not always attained. By connecting people with their source of energy wherever that may lie and by creating space, leaders can bring fulfilment within the reach of all. Leaders don't need permission; they just need to make it a priority. Has that time come for you?

Further reading from *The Leadership Hike*

Chapter 3 on fanning the flame of what inspires us.
Chapter 11 on helping people to grow.
Chapter 17 on clarifying vision and direction.
Chapter 19 on ways of encouraging buy-in.

Podcast with the author

In this podcast, Ollie Hart talks about how a sense of purpose and a drive to make a change propelled him into leadership roles. He discusses:

- How coaching skills can be used to help us become better leaders.
- How leaders can feel driven, how they can push to make things happen, and how this can impact on a team.
- Helping others to connect with what they care about.
- Coping with the 'grind': although leadership can be energising and uplifting, the hard part is keeping going. How might we do this?

CHAPTER

2

Faisal Bokhari

Faisal Bokhari works for NHS Greater Manchester Integrated Care as head of medicines optimisation for Tameside. Whilst working as deputy head of medicines optimisation and non-medical prescribing lead for Tameside and Glossop CCG, he was awarded the Greater Manchester Health and Social Care Partnership Leadership Champion Award, recognising his leadership and expertise on supporting other teams across the system, especially during the pandemic. He is currently working towards a doctorate in pharmacy with Keele University.

What have you learned about leadership and about people?

In my eight-year career as a pharmacist, I have learnt more about leadership through my interactions with other people than through leadership courses. However, both reflections on experiences and formal courses are important to have a holistic understanding of leadership. I've had managers over the years that adopted different leadership styles. In my early years, I was more welcoming of people who would take the time to empower me with skills to improve my practice and explain the rationale for their actions rather than not considering the impact their actions would have on me.

After completing various courses on leadership, my self-reflections were more meaningful as I was able to recognise different leadership qualities that underpin each style. People are instinctively different; however, there are qualities that we can reflect on and continuously improve. I believe it all begins through becoming emotionally intelligent, having an in-depth

DOI: 10.1201/ 9781003270492-3

understanding of yourself through proactive reflection, being self-aware and able to self-regulate, being empathetic and motivated, and more importantly, having an awareness of the effect your behaviours and speech have on others. Everyone has emotions, but how they display their emotions differs, and it is for a good leader to be able to recognise that and support the individual to appropriately regulate those emotions.

There are many theories around leadership which look at qualities and style, but these theories don't provide insight into the differences between effective and ineffective leadership. I have used two frameworks to continuously improve my skills and behaviours through reflection: the Royal Pharmaceutical Society Advanced Pharmacy Framework (Leadership cluster) and the NHS Leadership Academy – Healthcare Leadership Model (HLM). Around 3 years ago, I completed a self-assessment against the HLM, and I requested colleagues that I work with to complete the Healthcare Leadership 360 questionnaire which assessed my leadership qualities against nine fundamental dimensions: *leading with care, sharing the vision, influencing for results, engaging the team, evaluating information, inspiring shared purpose, connecting our service, developing capability, and holding to account.* Colleagues who completed the questionnaire rated me as a strong, well-balanced leader, which was positive to see and provided me with the confidence in the actions I took as a leader. However, I believe there is no such thing as a perfect leader; all leaders can make continuous improvements. I encourage and empower my team and colleagues to recognise that they are all leaders for the pharmacy profession within the daily roles they undertake. I am passionate about ensuring there is diversity of professional leadership across the workforce. This is part of the strategic vision for the pharmacy workforce group I co-chair for the Greater Manchester Integrated Care System. My role as a manager and leader is to recognise where improvements can be made and invest my time in my team so that they can also improve in the nine dimensions mentioned above. The wellbeing of my team is my first concern regardless of the task required; without a team it is difficult for a leader to produce intended outcomes.

Are there any things you might have done differently in retrospect?

In my final year of the MPharm undergraduate degree, there was an optional module on leadership and management which I didn't take, and on reflection, if I had opted for the module, I may have been better equipped to deal with my early career experiences. It would have helped me recognise and regulate my emotions. Ultimately, my reaction to someone else's action could have been better managed. I believe a leadership module should be a compulsory element within undergraduate degrees, equivalent qualifications, and training years to ensure early-year professionals in healthcare understand the different leadership qualities and styles their mentors or line managers may display, and subsequently, have the ability to reflect in a meaningful way and have a better understanding of how they react to those leaders.

There have been instances during my career when I have found it difficult to respond positively towards certain managers or mentors due to their style of managing and leading which affected my morale and subsequently my reaction. On reflection, I could have taken a proactive approach to ensure my morale was not affected through something I highly value now which is reverse feedback (i.e., feedback from the team members to the manager). I could have been more open and given my honest feedback rather than being apprehensive. The reason for being apprehensive was that I didn't see it happening and no one had ever told me that this was okay to do. I now believe this should be normal practice and it should be incumbent on leaders to create a culture in the workplace where this is normal. This is something I've had to normalise within my team. They now feel comfortable to approach me to tell me where I can make improvements and I regularly request their feedback. I believe this is a good way for leaders to verify your own self-reflection with their feedback.

How did it feel to be moving into a leadership role?

In October 2018, I moved into my first leadership role as deputy head of medicines optimisation. I remember reading the job description and feeling that it might be premature for me to apply given that I had only been qualified for 4 years as a pharmacist. However, I was able to recognise the potential development opportunities that the role would offer. Furthermore, I was able to recognise qualities of an effective leader in the current head of medicines optimisation. I saw this an opportunity to develop myself further and pull together everything I had learnt through previous roles under the mentorship of an experienced pharmacy professional. I remember my first meeting with my manager and felt overwhelmed seeing the long list of topics he had written down for discussion. At the end of the meeting, he said 'don't worry; we will work through things together and work at your pace'. Simple comments like this made me feel comfortable in the role but also made me recognise the importance of the scope of the role and responsibilities. There have been occasions where I have felt that I could have done better, or I didn't have the answers, but I believe that reflection following any interaction/occasion is absolutely key to continuously learn and improve yourself. I believe as a leader it is okay to acknowledge that you don't know everything, but it is the process a leader takes which is important to solve a problem.

Over the past 4 years in the role as deputy head of medicines optimisation, I have been more welcoming of leadership opportunities including chair of NW non-medical prescribing lead group and co-chair of the GM Pharmacy Workforce Group. The first question that comes to mind whenever an opportunity arises is, 'Can I do this?' One side of me always starts to overthink, but I have learnt to reflect on my thoughts systematically without rushing to conclusions. It is important to recognise your limitations but also important to continuously challenge yourself.

More recently, I have just taken up the role as head of medicines optimisation and I recall one of the interview questions: 'Leadership can be lonely. How will you deal with this?' I responded with 'It will only become lonely if you let it, especially if you don't reflect and identify the factors that will make you feel lonely. Informal daily reflections will ensure you can address any concerns. Utilising your network of peers to have regular discussions is absolutely key'. I have built good relationships with colleagues which has helped with having informal discussions. I have recognised that as a leader, it is important to create your own support network to ensure leadership doesn't become lonely.

What lessons/tips do you have for people stepping into a leadership role for the first time?

Everyone is different and your journey to becoming an effective leader will be different even though the principles or frameworks of leadership will broadly stay the same. You need to start with studying yourself through deep reflection and understanding your emotions in different interactions. Undoubtedly, there will be new situations that you may have never dealt with before, but it is the process of managing your actions as a leader and regulating those emotions. You will learn the most through your own reflections on personal experiences. Furthermore, it is important to substantiate your reflections through proactively asking for feedback with people you interact with regularly (e.g., 360 questionnaire or asking for feedback). Create a personal development plan where you identify gaps using SMART objectives. Remember to have confidence in your abilities and don't be afraid to seek out opportunities (e.g., influencing your colleague to reach a common goal). It is the small steps you take that will make the biggest difference to your development. As a leader, you will make mistakes, there will be challenges, and it is okay to ask for help or acknowledge that you made a mistake. The most important element following this is for you to reflect on this and see where things went wrong so you can continuously improve. As you start to get recognised for the impact you make to an individual or to an organisation, remember to stay humble!

Commentary

Faisal has been drawn to a leadership role relatively early in his career, despite admitting he decided against taking the leadership and management module during his undergraduate training. It seems many of us don't really understand leadership skills until we have had the chance to stand back and reflect. There appears to widespread belief in the myth that leaders are the people who know what should be done and stand at the front telling others what to do and how to do it. So, if we don't know everything, and don't feel comfortable telling others what to do, how can we possibly be leaders? If we then enter a workplace where this is exactly how the leaders behave, this perpetuates the myth and further discourages those with a different style to step up to lead.

For Faisal it seems a combination of his natural curiosity about the behaviours and style of those leading him, in combination with the opportunity to attend formal leadership training helped him to understand what leadership meant to him and how to apply this learning in the roles he undertook. He describes leadership theory and frameworks as well as formal feedback and personal reflection as being valuable in gaining insights into areas he may not have considered, improving his effectiveness as a leader.

This description reminds us of the theoretical ladder of competence. In this model of learning we move from unconscious incompetence (possibly still believing the myth that leaders are strong individuals who know what to do, and tell people to do it), through to conscious incompetence (an uncomfortable position when we recognise that what we are doing is not as effective as we hoped and that we need to learn to behave differently), to conscious competence (when we are actively applying new ways of being and reflecting on what works and why), and to the hope we will achieve unconscious competence (when leading effectively comes naturally).

Where do you feel you are currently at in your leadership development? Is it really as simple as this or do we move up and down the ladder in different situations?

Faisal describes his decision to apply for his first leadership role as a 'development opportunity' despite his concerns that he may not be ready for the job. Effective leaders often have a *growth mindset* rather than a *fixed mindset*. Individuals with a fixed mindset might use the phrase 'I'm not very good at that', whereas those with a growth mindset would say 'I'm not very good at that, yet'. If we feel we need to have all the skills/competence required of a role before applying, then we risk depriving ourselves of great opportunities for learning.

In healthcare you are likely to be given opportunities to step into new roles in the wider system outside of your frontline work. Many may feel these roles are beyond their level of competence. How often do you ask yourself, 'How can I grow, and what could I become capable of if I said yes to this opportunity?'

Leadership can often be as much about effective teamwork as it is about a single individual making things happen. Faisal recognises this in his desire to encourage his team to see that they are also leaders. His reticence during training to opt for the leadership and management module may come from a sense that learning about leadership and management before we are yet skilled in our professional field seems premature. It may be that exploring the key features of being a good team player could put individuals on the right path to becoming effective leaders, and this could be a useful addition to professional curricula especially in the early stages.

Faisal has clearly grasped opportunities to understand himself as the first step to working better with others, including a recognition of and attempting to manage his emotional responses to interactions. He describes this as an ability to self-regulate, something you could call 'keeping yourself in check'. Tools that might help us to gain both an understanding of our own preference, strengths, values, and style are often offered as part of leadership courses but are equally valuable in training about teamwork. So often we have significant 'light bulb' moments when we recognise our responses to situations are not universal, and by understanding our own perspective, we also recognise that others respond differently.

This is the first step to keeping ourselves in check. Whilst what we uniquely bring to a team should be celebrated, in some situations our strengths cast a shadow on others and interfere with getting the best outcome in a situation. For example, if we are naturally good at bringing conversations to a conclusion and are driven towards outcomes, we might get in the way of the more reflective team members who need time to process information before deciding how to respond. Sometimes we can be surprised by an emotion sparked by a work situation or comment from a colleague. An ability to recognise the feeling, hold it for long enough to decide what it means, before choosing the right response is not something that comes naturally to many of us, but it is something we can learn once we realise we need to.

Can you think of your own personal 'light bulb moments' when you realised something about yourself that was having an impact on others at work? How did you find out? This can sometimes generate strong emotions, not always positive, especially if you are prone to self-doubt. What did you do to manage these?

This takes us to our blind spots. How do we get to know what we don't know about ourselves and our impact on others? Faisal mentions how important he has found feedback and now encourages 'reverse feedback' from the people he leads, highlighting the importance of leaders generating a workplace culture that allows this to happen safely. Giving feedback is a complex skill. It is often seen as a one-way interaction when someone shares their perspective on the actions or behaviours of another with them to help them to change. In reality the situation is likely to be more complex, as the impact of a behaviour will differ among all those experiencing it, who will view it with their unique perspective. There will rarely have been a 'right way' and 'wrong way' of approaching things. Power imbalances are likely to impact how feedback is given and how it is received no matter how positive the workplace culture. It might be helpful to think of sense-making rather than feedback. When things don't go as hoped, discussing 'what happened there?' with people who are familiar with the context can help us to explore the dynamics of a group or a two-way interaction and uncover blind spots for both parties. Doing this authentically requires the humility and willingness to express our vulnerability that Faisal describes in his piece.

Think about the last work interaction that didn't go as well as you had hoped. Do you feel you fully understood the dynamics in the room and what went wrong? How could you generate an opportunity to find out?

Adaptive leadership theory describes the skill of 'moving from the dance floor to the balcony', meaning we can both be in the place where discussions are taking place and work is done, as well as watching the discussions and process from a metaphorical distance to see the dynamics of interactions and the impact of individuals (including our own) style on the responses of others and the overall outcome. This is a challenging skill to learn as well as being a hard habit to develop. Done well, it is very powerful and can build a leader's understanding of how to get the best out of their team; done badly, the leader might look remote and uncaring.

Next time you are involved in a meeting, try to participate, and observe what is happening at the same time and write down your reflections. If there is someone you trust who is also taking part, find time to talk through your thoughts. If you had become aware of dynamics that were negatively impacting the process of the meeting, what intervention may have been helpful?

Faisal's belief in the power of reflection and feedback, as well as his growth mindset and willingness to learn by grasping new opportunities, will help him achieve a greater understanding of self and others, something useful for all leaders.

Further reading from *The Leadership Hike*

Chapter 4 on understanding ourselves and using this understanding to develop deeper connections with others.
Chapter 14 on energising and motivating your team.

Podcast with the author

In this podcast, Faisal Bokhari talks about taking a first step into leadership even though you have all the skills at the outset, including:

- The importance of self-awareness and emotional intelligence in leaders and how to use these to be a better leader.
- How taking a first step into leadership doesn't mean you have all the skills at the outset; saying yes to opportunities can be an opportunity to grow and develop.

CHAPTER

3

Susan Bowie

Dr Susan Bowie is a GP from Shetland, a remarkable place with a remarkable community. She is not only a leader in her practice, developing it to a level that earned the Quality Practice Award from the RCGP, but she's a leader in the community, campaigning for services related to medicine such as end of life care and for wider issues like schooling. None of this has been possible without her dedication to people and to teamworking.

Leadership is something that I never imagined would be a big part of my career and never really anticipated or sought. Remote GPs, single-handed and in small rural practices, have had to assume the roles of leaders of their very small practices, and then subsequently teams, as practices have grown. And sometimes, leadership in their communities too.

I came to rural practice in 1984, as a novice GP. I had spent many summers as a student, working making kippers in a fish factory in Lerwick in Shetland, staying in 'gutters huts' and enjoying the camaraderie. We worked in teams at the factory, 'tintering' (putting kippers on 'tenterhooks'), chatting, and packing. We worked and played hard, and it was great exposure to the world of teamwork.

I came to GP too in a slightly roundabout way, which probably influenced my 'leadership style'. My mother worked as a cleaner in our own family GP practice on the south side of Glasgow. I remember the GPs were lovely, helpful, and looked after my parents in an exemplary fashion. However, a woman worked there as the receptionist, and though she was a great fun person, she was a terrifying receptionist. She made a huge impression on

DOI: 10.1201/ 9781003270492-4

me, and in the back of my mind later when I was employing staff at the surgery, she was there, the epitome of everything I didn't want in the staff.

Whilst there, waiting on my mum one weekend, raking among the bins in the back court, I found a very ancient brass microscope in its box, and this sparked a lifelong interest in science.

After medical school, I couldn't really decide which speciality to go in for, but eventually a chance encounter with a local GP brought about my wonderful training year in a relatively deprived part of eastern Glasgow. So much of what I learned about being a GP was learned there; about teamwork, and support for staff and colleagues, but mostly support and respect for patients and the difficulties life had to throw at them.

Subsequently after a spell in paediatrics, there came a 'sliding doors moment' and I chose GP. A peripatetic job supporting single-handed and small practices came up in Shetland. I thought I might do that for a year or so, and 38 years later I'm still here.

I was employed at first by the Health Board, gaining huge experience of different practices, and saw first-hand how things worked and what worked well. I was filled with admiration for the stoicism of the GPs and after a few years, as a young mother, I was appointed to my own practice. When I started there in 1988, it was on call 24 hours, no associate, and I had one member of staff. It was an enormous opportunity to build on what had gone before and shape the practice into our own. Other people joined our small band, mostly people with similar core values to me, people I could trust, were confidential, and could put our patients first.

In the late nineties, we had developed enough to consider applying for and achieving the Quality Practice Award, and subsequently we became a training practice. We had a super primary care manager and a very hands-on health board chief executive. They were immensely supportive and encouraged us to develop the practice. They came to see us regularly, and I learned much from them about how to take the team and the practice forward together with enthusiasm.

Not all of it was plain sailing. Our chief executive gave me nuggets of advice; 'It will pass' was one of them. However, I had two members of staff who were with me from the off, and who were able to help throughout, to put the brakes on when my enthusiasm got the better of me at times. Again, they shared my core values, and one of the first things we wrote when initially drafting the 'practice protocols' and leaflet was our practice ethos and principles, the practice charter, which we still give to patients.

Since the early 2000s primary care became more complex: new contracts and change in the 'out of hours', and it has felt sometimes like shifting sands, with change after change.

Steering a course through, sorting out the important from the unimportant, the must dos from maybes, has been tricky at times. I have tried to keep good longitudinal patient care at the heart of it.

From a personal point of view, the thing that kept me grounded, apart from my loyal team, was having a peer mentor, a GP from the Western Isles. We share ideas, talk through problems, and share protocols. We keep in touch regularly and phone each other several times a year. I've visited her practice and put into action the good ideas that I found there.

Along with changes in general practice came changes in organisation and primary care management over the years. It can sometimes feel that different folk are trying to reinvent the wheel every time there is a change. Drilling down to what's important, my thoughts are 'keep patient care at the most important heart of it and you won't go far wrong'.

Leadership doesn't just mean on a personal and practice level; I have found opportunities in the wider healthcare system. I realised that there was an enormous gap in care provision for those wishing to die at home or in a place of their choosing who sometimes didn't get their wishes. Given that women are able to choose home deliveries and have the right to a midwife to deliver them at home, I was sure that the dying should be able to access full palliative care in a place of their choosing. I pursued it with our Highland MSPs who agreed, and it went to the Scottish Parliament. This then progressed nationally in the UK through the Marie Curie organisation.

My thoughts on 'doing it successfully'

Be organised

In everything. Over the last 34 years, I've been pregnant three times and had three children; my husband, a journalist, occasionally worked away, and I had my mother to look after, plus the on-call. Surprisingly, rural practice worked well for me as I could organise the practice around the children and to an extent the family around the practice. My husband and later my children totally 'got it' and were unfailingly supportive. We lived close by. The on-call phone went with me to swimming galas. If I was on-call I needed a second someone to be at home with me, or to be able to come quickly if I got a call out, so I always had a backup plan to support the family.

Make sure you can manage 'yourself' too. The phone was always answered, the equipment in the car always updated (delegated to my practice nurses so I don't forget) and ready to go. A second doctor available and employed to give time off. Use of the hospital switchboard. Someone to make the meals at home and to be there for the children. Someone to help with housekeeping. Someone to support you if needed.

Hope for the best and prepare for the worst.

Ensure your family are happy

One of the main reasons we stayed long-term. My husband was able to (mostly) do the work he loved. We had fabulous child care and great granny care locally. We had wonderful local schools close by. Out of school activities for the children were excellent, and I made sure they didn't miss out because of 'mum's job'. I couldn't have done this job effectively without the support of my husband and family.

Have someone to talk to

It might be a member of your team, a colleague, someone in senior management, or a mentor. A trusted partner. A medical colleague. Or all of these. Bad things *will* happen, inevitably at some point, and you will need the support of someone to help get you through. My mentor is only a phone call away.

Lead from the floor

Lead your team, but learn from them too. Talk to them, support them, recognise their strengths, and ensure you praise them for what they do. Ensure you are a part of their team and are approachable always. Have coffee together and lunch. Share jobs. We are all in this together. Being able to cover each other's jobs and support each other has always been a big part of our team. Ensure they have everything they need to do their jobs properly and safely, whether it's training or adequate hours. Don't skimp.

Have practice meetings, and ensure your team know it's safe to air things. Don't overwhelm them. Introduce them to no-blame SEAs and make audit and self-reflection a part of every day. Make time to talk to them privately. Listen to concerns and back them up and if you have zero tolerance policies, mean it, and act on it if someone is unkind or nasty to your staff.

Pay them well, and ensure they get their pay rises and their proper time off and that their pensions are taken care of. Trust them to organise time off fairly amongst themselves, if you can, and bend over backwards to support them with time off for the good things in their lives.

Lead by example

Your practice is a place of work too. Ensure your behaviour is exemplary. Be kind to your patients and staff. Be trustworthy and be honest in everything. Be open and transparent.

Ditch things that don't really matter

No need to sit in a meeting for two hours for a chat if nothing is achieved or achievable. Now our meetings are pared back to the absolutely essential.

Look after your health and well-being

It seems obvious, but when you are putting others 'first' all the time, it's easy for your own health to take a back seat.

Sometimes bad things happen which we have no control of. In 2005 I had two serious high-speed car crashes and for about 3 years afterwards, post-head injury, my health suffered. Though able to work, I needed extra support and had to pare things back. My family and team supported me through it.

Make sure you take regular breaks. Ensure you have a good colleague who can take over, but ensure too that you have a hobby. I've had lots over the years including gardening and growing in our practice polycrub, music, and kayaking, but currently I'm a knitter and a sewer for my grandchildren mainly. Knitting can be incredibly meditative.

Delegate, and don't sweat the small stuff

You must have an excellent dispenser so that you don't have to do that all yourself. You must have an excellent member of staff trained in accounts so you don't have to do them yourself. You must have a great, well-organised administrator, who can ensure your car is always taxed and MOT'd, and so you don't have to worry about that. You will have a great practice nurse, happy to arrange the injectables, keep the treatment room stocked and your bags stocked. Let them do that themselves.

Where you can, delegate anything that you can, such as money and accounts. Admin jobs. Tax matters. You will have to organise most of the clinical jobs yourself and ensure that folk are not working beyond their competence, but if you delegate properly, it ensures things get done.

Routines

Stick to routines (written or unwritten protocols) and don't keep making changes unless they are beneficial. Routine means everyone knows where to find the defibrillator during an emergency or the paracetamol in the dispensary, and when you write your practice guide for your locum, they will find things in the right place too. Write these things down as protocols. They are really helpful for new members of staff coming during induction. Discuss any changes with your team.

Audit your performance and reflect on significant events

Do it as a team if you can. Learn with and from your team. Encourage others to do the same. Introduce these to students and trainees, too, and ensure your team understand that doing this is not about blame, it's about looking at and learning from what went wrong and at what we can do better.

Reflect and recognise what you don't do well, where your vulnerabilities lie

I realised that much as I was an enthusiast, I wasn't particularly great as a GP trainer. We had four failing GP registrars in a row, and I honestly got to the point that I didn't know what to do next with some of them. It stopped becoming enjoyable, and so I stopped doing it.

Formal appraisal should be useful for discussing these things.

Bad stuff

The thing that makes general practice so rewarding and different from other specialities for me is the almost unique longitudinal care and being able to maintain that to a high standard over a long period of time. Bad things will happen to your patients, possibly to members of your team, to colleagues, friends, and sometimes to your families. Some will get very sick, and some will die, and it will be much harder to cope with than you think. Having a strong team who can support you and each other at these times will be enormously important. The longer you stay in any area, the more friends you will make, and the more deeply you will feel the loss of colleagues, friends, and family.

In my own time as a GP I have coped with looking after my mother with dementia, significant family bereavements, illness and death of two of my members of staff, my own cancer, two head-on, life-changing road accidents, sepsis, and family illnesses. My good friend's daughter – who was a patient – died. Some losses will be difficult to bear. We must recognise our own vulnerabilities and frailties in this respect and find strength and help to carry on.

The most difficult things to deal with have been disputes amongst staff members and with staff members. It doesn't happen often, but when it does it's really very difficult for everyone in such a small team. Again, having fast easy advice was always helpful. My friends and mentor. The MDDUS at the end of the phone. The BMA. All absolutely essential.

Family

The advantages of our particular location, the community support and the access to technology meant that for both education and my husband's work, it was possible for the children to flourish academically and my husband to achieve success nationally and internationally. There are always ways of dealing with perceived issues of remoteness, and all it takes is willingness, a little money, and determination. If you can persuade the BBC to install a full digital broadcasting network so that a daily, national radio show comes to a remote part of the Shetland Isles, you can do anything.

Our family were secure, loved, and sustained a wonderful, stimulating lifestyle.

Leadership is sometimes about pushing the envelope. Looking for ways to make where you are, work. Place, family, community are key, and if you are content in a particular context, you can make the work, work.

It's about loving the work, and loving the people – your family, your community, your patients and staff. It is that love, I think, that has kept me here.

Commentary

People shape the place, at least that is the premise and hope of leadership, but the place also shapes the people. In Susan Bowie's evocative account of being a GP in Shetland, we have the impression of a remote land, shaping her and giving her a strong sense of her place in the community. Her 'place' comes across as being that of someone prominent but not arrogant. Her ability to face outward and serve, despite her reluctance to take a lead role, is the embodiment of humility, which we will now explore.

What does humility mean to you? It's often identified as an important attribute of effective leadership and a defining feature of great leadership. Is it something you recognise in yourself, and why might you nurture it?

The concept of humility can be difficult, perhaps because it has the reputation of a virtue that 'good' people have. However, because it helps people to feel better connected to us, it's worth trying to understand. What humility is *not* is being meek, weak, quiet, or lacking in confidence. It is not just the opposite of being arrogant or having too high an opinion of our abilities or importance. Rather, it is an attitude of appreciating ourselves and others that comes from understanding our place in the bigger picture. It is an open appreciation of who we are, warts and all, rather than who we might like to pretend we are. Humility is also accompanied by a generous recognition of the value of others. As a result, people warm to us and may offer their help even when they don't have to.

Susan's early life experience of working in a kipper factory helped her to gain this insight. It taught her the value and joy of teamwork, which she describes most vividly as a social activity, rather than one of rank, status, or control.

We can get a sense of our place by being in social groups or teams where we don't have higher status than others and can be ourselves. Where have you had that experience? What did you learn about yourself and how others saw you? What did you notice that others did better than you, and how did you feel about that?

We get another perspective on humility from its derivation, which is *humus*, or earth. This suggests that humility is a sense of being grounded, with a well-informed view of ourselves which is neither so inflated that we float above ground looking down on others or so unappreciative of ourselves that we go underground and bury our potential contribution. Interestingly, both over-estimations create problems because having too high a view of our worth feeds our self-interest, and having an inappropriately low view can feed our self-concern.

These mis-readings make us self-absorbed as leaders and less able to turn our attention outward towards our colleagues, where it is most needed. Where do you see that happening in your own life?

So, what does humility look like? It's not about presenting ourselves as humble, because that can be interpreted as 'virtue signalling'. It's more about how we *are* in terms of our attitudes and behaviour. These are shaped by a willingness to see ourselves truthfully, take responsibility for our mistakes, and accept ourselves honestly, especially in those areas where we know we have limitations.

If humility had a voice, it would say 'I don't have the answers, but *we* might'. That voice helps us not to make the mistake of trying to be self-sufficient and it leads us to greater openness and opportunity. We stop feeling bad that we are ignorant or incapable and become more willing to learn and adapt. In fact, evidence shows that humility can be a stronger predictor of performance than other attributes including IQ. Humility also stops us exhausting ourselves trying to keep up the appearance, for example, of expertise or infallibility. This wasted energy may not be apparent to us until we learn to change. Through our willingness to be vulnerable and to be human just like everyone else, humility connects us much more strongly to people. In reality, the more human we allow ourselves to be, the more believable we become.

The simple act of saying 'I don't know' is one of the hardest things to do. What holds you back from doing this? What would help you to do it in a way that doesn't undermine your self-confidence?

Susan brought 'not knowing' to the table and was not only open to ideas but grateful for the talents and contributions of others. Through humility, collaboration became a joyous necessity where the support received was acknowledged and rewarded.

Humility is not only good for leaders, but for everyone in the team because it is a force which, like altruism, gratitude, and forgiveness, binds people together. If our minds are more open, our attitudes will follow. We will invite help, listen, empower, and give believable praise in ways we may not previously have done. If we can foster generosity of spirit, we can acknowledge the value of others and compare ourselves with them more honestly. In these ways, the culture of a team is shaped. We move away from thinking of ourselves as autonomous individuals and recognise the richness of interdependency, where we share our resourcefulness and support.

How has your own humility opened up possibilities for yourself and especially for others? If it hasn't yet, what is standing in the way, and how could you address that?

Susan recognised the role she has played in setting the culture of her practice. She describes the importance of recognising the strengths of her team, praising what they do and sharing informal time such as breaks and lunch so that colleagues feel they are known as people and not just as employees.

Think about what happens where you work that helps people to feel valued. If this isn't happening as much as you feel it should, what changes might you suggest so that people know and appreciate each other's contributions better?

If humility is worth feeling, how can we nurture it? To get a more accurate estimation of ourselves, we can't just rely on our own perceptions but need to seek the type of feedback that we can act on. Making sense and giving appropriate weight to feedback is invaluable, and mentors and appraisers have an important role in shaping our self-esteem.

Susan found her mentor really valuable for support, ideas, and in reducing the sense of isolation that leaders often have. Who does this for you? How could you find one, and how do you think they could help you at this point in your life? How could they help you get a better sense of your strengths, vulnerabilities, and possibilities?

Humility helps us to be more effective because it guides us to a place where our talents are better used. Susan was able to see that her 'place' in the scheme of things was changing. As a result, despite her reluctance she put herself forward to be a leader, not for her own sake but because she saw that it was needed and that she had the capability. Many of us relate to this reluctance, but how many of us excuse ourselves in the hope or belief that someone else will accept the challenge? As well as stepping up, humility also helped Susan to step down when she recognised that her 'place' was not as a GP trainer, which was a role better occupied by others.

Humility helps us to put ourselves and our problems in proportion. Where do you feel you over- and under-rate yourself? With this in mind, what 'place' (a current role or task) would you move away from, and is there a place you recognise, perhaps reluctantly, that needs you?

With the many events and issues that she faced or endured, Susan says that she learned from the phrase 'It will pass'. Humility is at work here, too, because it helps us appreciate the limitations of our influence and capability. Things resolve with time, and our influence on outcomes may be important, but it is also limited. It is humility that helps us not to accept more praise or censure than is warranted.

Bad things will pass. How could you apply that knowledge to sustain yourself when you are suffering?

In a nutshell, humility helps us to feel comfortable with our own strength and with the strength of others without the toxicity of esteem issues like arrogance or jealousy getting in the way. As Susan's story shows, if we can plant that seed within ourselves, our whole community can blossom.

Further reading from *The Leadership Hike*

Chapter 5 on understanding the strengths that people have.
Chapter 7 on how we use our limitations to create opportunities for others.
Chapter 15 on helping the team to be their best.
Chapter 16 on how to adapt and be resilient, both personally and as a team.

Podcast with the author

In this podcast, Susan Bowie talks about her experience of working in the community, building effective teams, and how organisation and delegation can sustain a happy career and life, and discusses:

- How her leadership developed and embraced not just the practice but also the Shetland community.
- How to build an effective team with shared values and how to cope when people fall out.
- The importance of great organisation and delegation as the key to sustaining a happy career and life.

CHAPTER

4

Sheinaz Stansfield

Until 2023, Sheinaz Stansfield was a managing partner at Oxford Terrace and Rawling Road Medical Group, a multi-award-winning practice in Gateshead. She has also been director of transformation for Birtley & Central Gateshead PCN. She trained as a nurse and health visitor and has held senior management roles in commissioning and provision of health services in the Northeast. She became a practice manager in 2008 and supported the set-up of NHS Gateshead CCG and then was elected as the practice representative on the NHS Newcastle Gateshead CCG Governing Body. At a national level, she is a development advisor with NHSE Time for Care Team, Access Improvement Programme and board member of the NHS Confederation, which facilitates her passion for quality improvement, nurse and practice manager development, workforce redesign, patient involvement, and addressing health inequalities.

As I enter the winter of my career, I am reflecting on where I came from and where I ended up. I'm thinking about what I changed, and what I couldn't. Most importantly for those of you reading this – what is a leader? How, when, and why, did I become one?

Where I came from

My back story

I arrived in the UK on 10th November 1972. I was 9 years old. We fled Idi Amin's soldiers in the middle of the night, running from brutal killings in

DOI: 10.1201/ 9781003270492-5

the streets, homes being looted, and families being torn apart. All alone, my Mum brought her eight children to Greenham Common refugee camp.

My Dad, not being a British citizen, was sent to mainland Europe. He was able to join us 6 months later. We settled in Bradford, West Yorkshire. With a disrupted and strict Muslim upbringing, I left school with no qualifications, and was forbidden to pursue my dream of becoming a nurse. The future ahead was an arranged marriage and life as a housewife.

And so, once again, I left my home. At 18, estranged from my family, I came to Newcastle to train as an enrolled nurse. As the only Asian nurse, it was a lonely existence, and would only become lonelier with time.

I put myself through night school to progress my career, working my way through general nursing, occupational health, and health visiting. Working with voluntary organisations and community services, like my own experiences, I became aware of how needed minority ethnic, female voices were in care provision, not only because of gender bias, but also racial discrimination.

While doing my health visiting diploma, I was diagnosed with bowel cancer. The classic symptoms were brushed aside by my GP: 'You are a neurotic nurse and black women have a low pain threshold'. Those words still haunt me, and later in my career they would drive my passion to ensure equality and inclusion for those I would serve and also strive to deliver the highest quality of care for all my patients.

My faith in the NHS was stolen from me. And so, nearly, was my career. I fought to remain on my health visiting course, being told by managers that I shouldn't continue. Against the odds, within 4 weeks of surgery I returned to my studies qualifying with my year group.

I only lasted a year in health visiting. My interest was in health promotion and prevention, but I was pushed into duties that facilitated box-ticking and made no difference to the well-being of my families. With no influence at operational level, I took the risk of applying for and was appointed into my first management post.

In the hope of having more influence in better patient outcomes, I became one of the NHS' first BAME Commissioning Managers, writing the first strategy for commissioning services for BAME groups, and embarked on an MBA. The focus then was on empirical evidence. Qualitative approaches, leadership, and culture were not considered in the NHS, with very limited literature available on the subject. My MBA dissertation looked at the barriers to patient participation in primary care. I started to develop an interest in organisational culture, with a focus on compassionate, inclusive, and distributed leadership, in the hope of finding better opportunities to grow and flourish as a leader.

Many primary care trusts nationally used my work to inform their patient and public involvement strategies, but I felt this was in a transactional fashion to attain rewards, as is the way of the target culture of the NHS. My intent was to create a transformational environment, where discretionary effort enabled change and improvement in care, through engagement, co-design, and partnership.

Twenty years in commissioning, I feel I made no visible difference to patients. There was organisational change almost every 2 years, and I wandered blindly into numerous unfulfilling management roles and an isolated career path.

I suffered from change fatigue, compounded by five major operations related to my initial surgery. A simple surgical procedure went wrong, necessitating a lengthy recovery period. With more organisational change looming, I was the first in the organisation to be made redundant, on my return to work.

My union tried to support me, but I did not have the strength or will to pursue a claim. The NHS felt like a toxic place, and with no other BAME people around me, my work colleagues seeing but not supporting me, I was isolated, in pain, and had no fight left. I asked for my last 6 months to be seconded to Gateshead PCT where I would implement clinical commissioning. Feeling personally and professionally let down by the NHS, I decided to leave in pursuit of a career in academia. On my last day at work, at a time in time out educational session, my clinical director said:

> It's Sheinaz' last day with us today. The HR arrangements will not allow us to keep her, but I will do all I can to bring her back at the earliest opportunity.

I had the most wonderful summer holiday with my children that year. On the 28th day I received a call to return as a consultant in the role I had vacated. Within a year, I was asked to apply for that same job. With a supportive leadership team, I was very successful in setting up clinical commissioning in Gateshead. However, with further organisational change, triggered by the 2012 Health and Social Care Act, I felt this was no longer the place for me. I decided to pursue that PhD again.

Where I ended up

A chance meeting and disagreement with a GP resulted in me taking a job as a practice manager for 18 months. Connecting directly with my personal values and motivation, these words convinced me:

> Mrs Stansfield, we want someone who will challenge us, someone who will question us and someone who will bring complementary skills and be outward-looking for our practice.

Fourteen years later, I realise that was the best career decision I ever made. Coming to Oxford Terrace and Rawling Road Medical Group, I found my 'tribe'. Partners here helped me be the best version of myself. We had a shared purpose and very clear joint strategic direction. They enabled me to enact all the leadership competencies I felt important, I had influence without the need to compromise on patient care, because quality and patient safety were at the heart of everything we do. I was allowed the financial resources and support for my team to deliver excellent patient care, with a compassionate, inclusive leadership style.

The traditional culture in general practice has facilitated a command-and-control management style based on rewards and punishments. Convincing the team that I was a leader and not a typical 'old-guard' manager was a challenge in the early days. Before long the team would follow, embracing a distributed leadership style working together towards the same shared purpose. We now have a culture of continuous quality improvement (QI). Moving from the traditional single 'hero leader' we have a distributed complementary leadership team. We have cascaded QI skills, enabling a compassionate and inclusive culture throughout the team, with partners enacting the behaviours cascading them across the organisation.

Developing a passion for QI by joining the NHS England Sustainable Improvement Faculty, started my journey of self-discovery. An important development then was starting to understand my motivational value system, through relationship intelligence and behavioural theory; this was highly illuminating, helping me understand myself and adjust my approaches to make interactions and relationships more effective.

Where others saw danger, I saw opportunity; where some saw risk I saw reward, my motivation was all about taking risk to make my own luck: 'go big or go home'. I succeeded in a world where opportunities are constantly available, but others failed to take. Relationships with peers became difficult. My behaviours, whilst motivated by the need to collaborate, work together, share, and spread achievement, were perceived by others as competitive, self-serving, gambling, and questioning the status quo. A leader needs followers; I had none.

Immersed in a world of QI, particularly 'the human dimensions of change', I found new confidence, enabling me to use relational theory to build better relationships. I was for once in my career surrounded by a team that lifted as we climbed, critical friends around me, using feedback and making use of opportunities to suit me as a unique individual leader. Understanding how others perceived me, coupled with improved self-awareness helped me to build better relationships, become a more compassionate inclusive leader with a growing followership, sharing personal power to influence change.

Using my strengths of task accomplishment, achieving results, a strong desire to set goals, take decisive action, and claim earned rewards attributed to transforming my practice following a merger. Winning 15 awards in one year resulted in award ceremonies, newspaper articles, and radio and TV appearances, propelling me to a national platform and having now the power to influence national policy on population health and new models of care. My nursing and leadership skills entwined beautifully to plan and deliver excellent patient care.

I hadn't ever in my wildest dreams thought I would ever find myself in such a position. None of this would have been possible without the support of amazing GP partners, who offered me an equal partnership. I learned the mastery of anticipating the needs of my practice, my team, and practice population, looking for and finding opportunities during times of adversity, serving the people I lead and working with them to overcome hardships or challenges.

My team and our patients are the experts. Better self-awareness has taught me to deflect attention away from myself, encouraging others to use their voices. My role as a leader is to hold value in the team with fairness, equality, and equity empowering people to share ideas, collaborate, and shine as one.

What I changed

Equality, diversity, and inclusion (EDI)

In my practice and the Time for Care teams, I am immersed in environments that allow the exploration of differences, in a safe and nurturing way, so that we may understand each other better, be more tolerant, and celebrate the unique differences we bring to the team and our work. What does this mean to me?

- Diversity is the act of celebrating difference, it's about empowering people by respecting and appreciating what makes them different, in terms of age, gender, ethnicity, religion, disability, sexual orientation, education, and national origin.
- Inclusion is about embracing these differences, allowing opportunities, listening to, valuing everyone's contribution, which would lead to:
  - Equality, treating everyone the same, and everyone receiving the same benefits
  - Equity, which bolsters diversity and inclusion by treating people with fairness and justice.

Having encountered much adversity in my personal and professional lives, I hold these values deep inside my heart. I use each of the negative experiences as an opportunity to learn and make it better for those I serve. My 'why' is to look after people, care for them, inspire them so that together we can make the world a better place one thing at a time.

What is a leader?

In the NHS we have many leadership development programmes. We give people big titles, offices, status, and position; we have a pathway for those who have been talent-spotted to attain these things. If you show up and impress the right people, you may end up on that pathway.

Until recently, these pathways were not accessible to those working in general practice. Attempts to scale up general practice have failed without the necessary personal or organisational development infrastructure. People attain leadership positions because they put their hands up, their position, title, or status, not always on merit. This approach grows managers who take charge but do not give charge. Without the right leadership competencies, scaling up remains an unattainable aspiration.

Training and titles do not make leaders. To me, leadership is a way of being with, and connecting with people. It is about inspiring, supporting, nurturing, and empowering others – holding their hand as they become the best possible versions of themselves. Leaders have empathy and a desire to improve things, and then listen to and rally with their people, together moving towards a shared purpose.

My leadership hikes

I have no hints and tips to share, but only gifts handed down to me by others, as our paths crossed, on my journey of self-discovery.

My first exposure to a true inclusive leader was in my first management role. There I experienced a leader who supported and helped me trying to find my way as a nurse in a command-and-control NHS commissioning and provider environment: an amazing woman, innovative, dynamic, and courageous. When she was leaving, I asked how I could repay the support she had given me. She said, 'Pay it back to others, Sheinaz'.

Two GPs, now my partners and muses, believed in me, taking me in during my darkest hours, allowing me to remain in the NHS, being the best possible version of myself. They put me back together, nurtured and supported me quietly. Other partners are equally important, and together we bring Patrick Lencioni's five dysfunctions of a team to life:

- We trust each other implicitly, allowing us to be vulnerable with each other taking risks together.
- We have open healthy debate, constructive conflict, and trust each other to speak our opinions without retribution.
- We avoid artificial harmony, value healthy conflict, opposition, and disagreement; this enables commitment, speaking with one voice, and innovating courageously.
- We hold each other to account.
- We have and celebrate collective results.

With this strong foundation as an organisation with a clear sense of shared purpose, we have grown exponentially as individuals and as an organisation in the 14 years of being part of a clinically led and managerially enabled organisation. This has carried us into a trusting, collaborative and successful primary care network of three practices.

As I attended my first NAPC conference, the host told me I could not do things alone; I needed an organisation behind me. The National Association of Primary Care became that organisation. From my first year as a practice manager, they included me into the fold and opened opportunities for me as part of their innovation network. They helped to me test and share new developments initially as a committee member and then executive board member, giving me a platform and a voice. I used this initially to articulate the need for Practice nurse (GPN) development, and they supported me to hold the first conference for GPNs. That transformed into the nursing voice, and best practice in nursing was born. My ambition remains to have a funded comprehensive competency framework, development programme, and career structure for both GPNs and practice managers. I influence this now as an NHS Confederation board member.

When the leadership commission was set up, I complained that out of 250 members there was no primary care involvement. A national leader heard my plea and set up a primary care leadership summit. She asked me: 'Do you feel different? Do you feel out of place and uncomfortable all the time? That's because you are a deviant leader'. I joined her on the first Primary Care Vanguard programme as the only practice manager. My journey in QI began here.

I was introduced to the Sustainable Improvement Team and initially as a faculty member, giving me the opportunity to share and spread all the innovation we had tested in practice. Taking a QI approach to my practice work freed up 1, then 2, and then 3 days of my time. I now work with the Time for Care programme, and QI is the strong foundation my leadership decisions are based on.

In this team I was privileged to have my first formal mentor. Being a constant critical friend, she pushed me so far outside my comfort zone, and I barely recognise the woman I have become. She nurtured and taught me much of what I know about QI. Alongside others in the team, I developed a passion for demand and capacity management, workforce redesign, reliable design to address safety in general practice, and so many other QI tools, and most importantly, to be courageous, be more me, and believe in myself.

This team keeps me resilient, being critical friends, mentors, and teachers, affording me opportunities for personal growth that I had never deemed possible. Their compassionate and inclusive leadership sees beyond the black woman into the person that I am. I often say to them, 'I was born in the NHS but made in the Time for Care team'.

Opposition is an opportunity

Those who know me say that courage and passion are the golden threads to my life and work story. I see opposition as an opportunity for innovation and find it healthier than artificial harmony. I don't like conflict, but I detest artificial harmony. To this end, I will challenge and oppose in the hope of healthier debate, openness, and to build trust. I understand now that this has been the cause of some professional isolation at points in my career, but it is a price worth paying.

How, when, and why did I become a leader?

I have never had any formal leadership training, never been on a pathway or until recently had a formal leadership mentor; my support has been round QI. Also, I have never had the desire to be a CEO. I wanted my feet to always be firmly attached to the ground, doing the things that were important to me, with behaviours that allowed me to be true to myself. I didn't crave or want status or position. However, influence is something I always knew I needed if I was to ever make a difference. Leading with influence has allowed me to create a space for true inclusion and collaboration, giving away power. I delegate, mentor, support, and nurture team members so that we can achieve team goals together.

My leadership hike has taken many twists and turns. I feel very fortunate that many empathetic, brave, and accessible leaders crossed my path, leaving me a small gift as our lives touched. They gave, but never asked anything of me in return. Their words ring still in my ears as I try to emulate what I saw in them and what they taught me.

I'm not sure when I become a leader. I think I have always had the attributes to be a leader – we all do – but without the necessary opportunity to lead and influence, I drifted aimlessly.

Finding my tribe, the right situation to lead without fear of failure or retribution allowed me to create an environment for my team that I would have wished for myself, a place to be creative, innovative, solution, and quality focused, delivering excellent care for those we serve. I often say, as a practice manager I nurse by proxy; by caring for my team, I get to care for 17,500 patients every day.

What a privileged and wonderful journey I have travelled. One of the most important things I have learned is to believe in myself and surround myself with people who will support and enable me to grow and feel safe to make mistakes in a culture that values diversity and celebrates and embraces difference in us all.

We need to learn how to lead through others; this has become a particular strength. I strive to systematically lift people up to lead; spotting potential, I harness and nurture it, growing my own without the necessary leadership development in primary care. It is important that we identify talents and give people support and courage to bring it out and realise it. People say my passion is infectious and people mirror it, fuelling even more courage and passion in those around me, and thus my followership grows.

Conclusion

Compassionate, inclusive leadership are not qualities I see in many of those at the top of the NHS. Our current leadership can be toxic in culture and style, an iron grip that commands and controls.

In general practice we have hero leaders, with individual competences, behaviour, and style. The senior partners and now PCN clinical directors set the tone, and for those without the necessary access to a different way of being emulate the behaviours at the top.

That said, as individuals we have a choice about how we set the tone for and with those we serve. Michael West's work on compassionate and inclusive leadership could not be timelier, as we handle to aftermath of the ravaging pandemic. Organisations where leadership is visible everywhere embraced by an empowered team.

Throughout my career I have seen much adversity but always taken responsibility for myself, seeking opportunities where I could. This may at times come across as a powerful assertive personality, driven by lack of confidence and self-awareness, an approach that did not always win friends or followers. But, until I was able to understand myself better and become cognisant of how others perceived this, I did not realise how much it affected my relationships. This learning along the way came into play when the time and place were right for me. Feeling more confident now, having influence I can be compassionate, caring, and true to my values and principles.

As I slowly ebb into the winter of my career, I feel accomplished, I am enough, and I have been given more gifts than I could have ever hoped for. My aspiration now is to share these gifts as I touch other lives, moving into the next chapter of my life.

Commentary

Sheinaz's career has taken a rocky route, and she is clear her final destination made it worth the journey. She is an individual who has discovered her significant power, and this power appears to have developed as a response to adversity in her work as well as her personal life, including overcoming significant health challenges that were initially disbelieved by her own healthcare provider. It seems experiencing injustice and personal health challenge have acted as if to coil a spring from which she has gained the energy to drive herself forwards, moving from roles when it becomes clear this energy is not being well spent. There is a sense that the low expectations of others helped Sheinaz to find the energy to prove them wrong. She acquired credibility through qualification (nursing, health visiting, and her MBA) as well as awards and accolades for her achievements. Many of us are driven either by injustice we have experienced ourselves or witnessing this for others.

Consider the source of your own drive. Is it enough to sustain the energy you need for the work you do? If you are driven by a need to prove others wrong, how might this impact your leadership once you feel you have proved yourself?

Sheinaz highlights so well the importance of context with regard to how much we can achieve. In the wrong environment it is hard to flourish, no matter how skilled or driven we are. Once she found colleagues who valued what she brought to the team, she could apply all she had learned about leadership, organisational culture, and QI to take the practice from strength to strength. She found a place where she could be vulnerable, where she could make mistakes and learn, rather than be pilloried. In this environment she found her power and put it to use.

Do you feel you might not be able to put your skills and passions to best use in the environment where you work? If so, do you need to move on, or are there things you can do to influence the culture and context of your workplace?

Sheinaz's drive and passion, as well as her willingness to take risks and 'make her own luck', are clear strengths. Our strengths can sometimes cast a shadow on others, and Sheinaz's realisation that her leadership behaviours were negatively impacting her relationships with peers, and that she was perceived as being competitive and self-serving, must have been a salutary experience. The challenge of making the most of the power we have to influence and achieve, whilst at the very same time helping our colleagues to do the very same thing, must be one of the greatest leadership challenges. Power can cloud our ability to notice what goes on around us. Strong drive makes us less sensitive to what goes on in the shadows, and it's not always easy to know if this is happening. Sheinaz had the opportunity during the improvement leaders programme to take part in a reflective exercise to explore her strengths and motives using the Strength Deployment Inventory. She has described this as a 'light bulb moment', when she started to recognise that her strengths, whilst useful in a leader, needed to be used alongside an ability to anticipate the thoughts, feelings, and actions of others and to make choices about her own words and actions to ensure they empower rather than diminish others. In a similar way, if one of our strengths is attention to detail, we could sap the energy out of a meeting by failing to acknowledge and appreciate those who are keen to get started on a project.

Think about the people you know in leadership positions. What have you noticed about their strengths? Consider if their strengths have a negative impact on your own thoughts, feelings, or behaviours. How might your own strengths be casting a shadow on others?

Sheinaz's achievements have been externally recognised by the many awards she and her team have won. Awards can give a sense of satisfaction to those involved and help team positivity and cohesion along with a feeling it has all been worthwhile. External validation can give leaders and teams the energy to keep going, especially when things are particularly difficult.

Awards, however, can have some negative impacts. Sometimes they result in overconfidence and a subtle sense of superiority, which might negatively impact future performance and decision-making. Winners can feel an increased pressure to maintain high levels of performance and success, which can lead to stress and burnout. Winning awards can sometimes generate jealousy and resentment among peers or competitors, leading to strained relationships and decreased collaboration.

'Winning teams' may attract those drawn by the spirit of competition rather than collaboration; how would you guard against this?

In some situations, a focus on winning awards can cause individuals or organisations to neglect other important aspects of their work, such as employee well-being. These negative impacts can often be mitigated or avoided through awareness, thoughtful management, and communication.

Some people thrive more on external validation than others. How much do you know about what motivates your team? If you are someone who doesn't value external validation yourself, could this mean you forget to openly celebrate the achievements of others, including nominating them for awards they might value? How would you ensure that your team is valued for what it has achieved rather than for what it has won?

Sheinaz describes how she has developed a distributed leadership style during the time she has been a GP practice manager and managing partner. Distributed leadership is an approach where decision-making and leadership responsibilities are shared among multiple individuals within an organisation, rather than being dominated by a single person or a small group. In this model, leadership is a shared responsibility with collective decision-making, innovation, and problem-solving, and there is a focus on developing leadership capacity at all levels of the organisation. The advantages are clear. People working with the organisation can gain a greater satisfaction in their role if they have some control over the decisions. Problems start to become less of something for the leader to solve, and more a collaboration of problem-solvers working together. For it to work, leaders need to act with humility and open their hearts to the strengths of others. Distributed leadership is a particularly difficult thing to achieve for leaders who have a clear vision of what they feel needs to happen in their organisation, and a strong sense of accountability. Distributing leadership can sometimes result in a lack of cohesion and direction with the potential for misunderstandings and inefficiency, at least at first until the system embeds, and so leaders may need to be courageous to persist with the approach.

If distributed leadership is a model you are striving for in your own organisation, it might be valuable to think about how you will know if you have achieved it. If decisions are made in meetings when you aren't present, does your team check that you agree before proceeding with any changes? If this is the case, maybe there is something about your words and behaviour that results in others feeling they don't truly have the right to make changes without you. How much do you trust the people and the process?

Sheinaz is coming towards the end of her career as a healthcare leader and so can look back on her journey with everything she has learned with honesty and humility. She now focuses on handing over the baton, ensuring those she leaves behind have the confidence to step into her shoes.

Further reading from *The Leadership Hike*

Chapter 7 on understanding the impact of the shadow side of our strengths.

Chapter 11 for how to develop the leadership skills of others, including effective delegation
Chapters 22 and 23 on how to use quality improvement methods to make a difference.

Podcast with the author

In this podcast, Sheinaz Stansfield describes her career from healthcare assistant to nurse and then on to leadership roles driven by a need to help communities and understand population health needs. She discusses:

- The importance of understanding our strengths as well as the things we are less good at so we can build an effective team
- How understanding that your strengths, if overplayed, may have a negative impact and how we can use this understanding to be better leaders.

CHAPTER

5

Carey Lunan

Carey is a GP who has worked with marginalised groups over many years and combines the compassion she feels for individuals with the drive to improve the lives of large and diverse communities. She has had several national roles including chair of the RCGP in Scotland. She has also been chair of the Scottish Deep End project, comprising GPs working in some of the most deprived communities in Scotland. Leading on from this, Carey took the position of senior medical advisor on health inequalities to the Scottish Government.

I must confess I've always had antibodies to the word 'leadership'. I felt it related to something or someone 'other' than me, but I have slowly come to recognise, over the course of my career, (which has developed organically without any 'game plan'), that leadership is something that we *all* do – when we role model, when we speak out, when we influence, when we make change. Leadership happens at many levels, and it's just that some roles are more formally recognised than others.

I have always had a 'love-hate' relationship with medicine as a career. I have found being a doctor the most enormous privilege, in terms of the trust that people place in me, and the stories that they share, often at the darkest times in their lives. The quality of my relationships with people, with colleagues and with the world, matters a lot to me, as does a working environment that offers a sense of hope, autonomy, and purpose. Conversely, when these things are threatened or constrained, I can feel disillusioned, trapped, and disconnected. I have worked as a doctor in the NHS for 25 years and have found my home in medicine as a general practitioner, working within a deprived community in Scotland. I have learned

DOI: 10.1201/ 9781003270492-6

more from my interactions with patients and their families, and through conversations with trusted colleagues, than I could ever have learned at medical school. I have come to realise that all the changes that I tried to make over the course of my working life have had the same motivation at their core: create the conditions for quality relationships.

I qualified as a GP in 2003, but with training completed, I didn't feel ready, and I wanted to keep learning. Accepted onto a postgraduate fellowship, I completed an MPhil in law and ethics in medicine at Glasgow University, developed skills in teaching at undergraduate and postgraduate levels, nurtured an interest in qualitative research and had my first experience of 'deprivation medicine' in Craigmillar, Edinburgh. My dissertation topic reflected on personal autonomy, advanced decision-making, and a review of the legal frameworks that existed to support patients and clinicians. It may sound dry, but it was a deeply personal topic for me at the time. My mum was dying of a brain tumour, and as a family we had not had the opportunity, or the foresight, to explore her wishes for care. At the age of 57, having lost her capacity, we found ourselves in the difficult position of having to make decisions on her behalf, and as the eldest child and the doctor, this largely fell to me. I felt helpless and overwhelmed – and driven to find a better way for families in our situation, and for those who had lost their autonomy and voice. She died in 2005, and this personal heartache and grief possibly prompted me to wish for better communication skills in medicine and more of the 'What if?' type conversations to be available as part of good care. I was also struck by the profound impact of simple acts of kindness and compassion. My sisters and I, visiting mum for the last time, were taken outside by one of the nursing assistants on the ward. She sat us down, made us a cup of tea, listened to us, and said to me, 'This will make you a better person'. She was right, I think. This interaction, with its simplicity, its honesty, and its bravery, has stayed with me throughout my career.

These early experiences influenced the kind of doctor I wanted to be, and the kind of medicine that I wanted to practice. My first local leadership role was in anticipatory care planning, and this gave me the opportunity to explore and develop ways of supporting patients, their families, and the clinicians looking after them. The premise was simple: support clinicians to have proactive care-planning conversations with their patients, record these conversations, and share them with those who needed to be aware of them when the time came. Of course, the reality was far from simple: a cultural antagonism to talking about death and dying, clinicians feeling underconfident and unprepared to have these difficult conversations, systems that we work within not readily supporting information continuity, but – most crucially – simply lacking the time needed to do this well.

I worked with others to create and deliver learning resources for clinicians, to improve the information-sharing software we had available, and to raise awareness with politicians of the need for an adequately resourced workforce to allow the time and space to do this important work.

It was during this time, when I was also working as a GP appraiser, that I began to develop a curiosity about the 'interfaces' of care, where patient journeys traverse different complex systems. At these transition points, and especially between primary and secondary care, things often seemed to break down and errors occurred, sometimes with devastating consequences. Colleagues shared with me examples of where recorded wishes had not been followed around unwanted resuscitation, resulting in distress for families and clinicians, because of breakdowns in information-sharing systems. These dysfunctional interfaces were damaging for patients, for system efficiency and for inter-professional relationships. I began to explore ways that we could better understand and share learning from these interface breakdowns in a way that supported both sides and avoided a culture of blame.

The NHS, with its tendency towards 'silo-working', especially in times of stress, doesn't routinely create the conditions for us to see and understand the bigger picture, or to share learning more widely to bring about change. As GPs, I think our generalist training encourages us to think in this way. I asked practices if they would be willing to share anonymised examples of 'significant event analysis' discussions where interface breakdown was an identified theme. I analysed the themes from 70 of these, providing the data that I needed to be able to articulate what seemed to be going wrong, and to persuade those in positions of power that priority needed to be given to improving our interface between primary and secondary care.

Some conversations were more successful than others, and I learned that it was important to try and establish at an early stage what motivated the person I was trying to persuade, and what my 'levers' were in trying to achieve this. Some were persuaded by safety, some by efficiency, some by improving patient and clinician experience, and some by reducing the potential for complaints and litigation. After many months of meetings and conversations, it was agreed that we could establish a dedicated interface group in our area, bringing together a small, selected group of representative and influential GPs and hospital doctors on a regular basis to try to understand why things broke down at the interface and what could be done to improve them. Having co-chairs from both primary and secondary care felt important, as did an agreed set of principles around how we sought consensus. I was the primary care co-chair for the first 2 years, and being a part of that group reminded me that our collective voice is far more powerful, and that we risk losing that collective voice at our peril and that of our patients.

I think that sometimes GPs can feel alienated and remote from colleagues in hospital medicine, and this can be amplified in times of stress, or fuelled by unbalanced reports in the media. In addition to tackling the thorny interface issues of the day (referral pathways, discharge planning, shared care prescribing, and much more), the real achievements were in the rediscovery of our sense of common purpose: to provide high-quality patient care, facilitated by mutually respectful and supportive interprofessional relationships within functional systems. I took the learning from this group into a national role with the Royal College of GPs as their first national interface lead. Making the case to prioritise the interface, which can seem nebulous, difficult to define, 'own', or change, is an ongoing challenge.

An unexpected ally arrived in the form of the Covid pandemic. With the growing realisation of the enormity of the challenge facing the NHS, and the need to work together to protect the whole system, those boards that had functioning interface groups quickly demonstrated their worth. Pre-existing relationships of collaboration and trust, established mechanisms for rapid communication and sense-checking, and a familiar need to ensure that changes in one part of the system didn't have unintended consequences on other parts of the system, were invaluable.

In 2017, nearing the end of my interface role, it was suggested to me that I consider applying for chair of the RCGP in Scotland. A role known for its intensity and its high profile, this would be the biggest challenge to date of my career, and in honesty, it wasn't an easy decision for me to make. I knew that I could (to a certain extent) plan for the practical demands, but I wasn't so sure about the psychological ones. As the leader of an organisation that also had expectations around corporate identity and political neutrality, would I 'fit'? Was I too idealistic? Too stubborn or impatient for change? Would I be able to compartmentalise when I really cared about something that wasn't achievable? Would I be at risk of burnout, trying to achieve everything I wanted to do? I was also aware that I would be taking on the role at an extremely challenging time for the profession, at the peak of negotiations around a new GP contract that was already dividing opinion and testing relationships. After much soul-searching and research, I decided I would apply and subsequently dedicated the next 3 years of my life to the role. My first 6 months focused on listening, observing, and building relationships. I had much to learn about the politics, the personalities, and what was required and expected of me, and the learning curve was steep.

I have always placed value on 'feelings intelligence' and intuition, and the relationship-building focus paid off (I think). I find I can naturally connect with people and can 'read a room' quickly. I invest personally in relationships with colleagues, and I like to be prepared and well-thought through for the stuff that is important to me. I dislike conflict, but I won't avoid it. I will always try to collaborate and seek consensus when I can, whilst accepting that sometimes that is not possible. I can live with that, if the disagreement is handled with integrity, kindness, and congruence with what I believe to be the right thing to do. Seeking consensus where possible has made taking on the occasional role of 'critical friend' easier.

My 3 years as chair of the RCGP in Scotland were a roller coaster ride of emotional highs and lows, with the final year during the first lockdowns of the Covid pandemic. I was committed to doing the very best I could during that time, for the profession and for patients, and one of the great privileges of the role was the opportunity to progress personal areas of interest. I chose building interfaces, growing the GP workforce, and improving practitioner well-being and the role of general practice in addressing health inequalities.

In choosing health inequalities, I found a way of connecting the experience of my frontline clinical work with my leadership work. They informed and complemented each other. From early on in my medical career, I found I was drawn to working with more marginalised groups and supporting those who cared for them. A few years after qualifying as a GP, I had moved from my first partnership to a salaried role, caring for those experiencing homelessness. The years working as part of that team were life-changing. My medical training to date could not have prepared me for the complexity, the intensity, and the enormity of the task at hand. At first, I was overwhelmed. I felt professionally useless with what I felt able to offer my patients, whose hierarchy of needs was focused solely on survival. I was unaccustomed to the complex psychodynamics at play in the consulting room, where patients I was seeking to care for frequently appeared to sabotage and reject my efforts.

At the point when I was questioning whether I could continue, I was offered a lifeline, and a way to turn the challenge I was facing into learning and growth. An opportunity arose to establish a reflective practice group for the GPs in the team. For one protected hour per month, with a skilled facilitator, we talked about the consultations we were finding difficult, which we were struggling to understand, and which generated the 'emotional labour' of our work. Over those 5 years, I came to understand many things: how the childhood adversity and dysfunctional caring relationships of many patients played out in the consulting room when care was offered; how a lack of understanding of these dynamics could result in compassion fatigue and a 'splitting' of teams; and how re-enactment of these power dynamics within the doctor-patient relationship could lead to the 'rejection' of 'non-engagers'. Those hours spent in reflective practice were, for me, professionally lifesaving and forged a deeper understanding of what it means to provide a trauma-informed service.

I began to approach my consultations differently, to accept that 'care' for many of our most vulnerable patients starts with building trust, being consistent and kind, and listening. I had to challenge my medic ego and what needed to be achieved in those spaces and develop a greater understanding of what achievement actually meant. With that came a humility for the burdens that many of my patients were carrying, and an increasing realisation that many of the destructive behaviours that ultimately shortened lives were driven by a fundamental lack of choices, and a need to manage both physical and psychological pain. I realised how ill-prepared we are with our current undergraduate and postgraduate training for working in these circumstances, and that this needs to change if we are to sustain compassionate practice and avoid burnout.

The learning and insights I discovered through reflective practice work have, I believe, driven me to strive for a more psychologically informed leadership style in several ways. I have found that I naturally ask in challenging situations: What is the need that is being expressed here? How is that need driving behaviour? What is the countertransference I am experiencing? I now treat these situations like a challenging consultation and break it down and analyse it in the same way. I have always been sensitive to what is *not* said in any interaction and am now more able to process that in a useful way. Consciously or subconsciously, we all bring our own histories and trauma into our interactions with other people, and effective leadership for me is primarily about understanding human behaviour, motivation, and potential – and building relationships of trust and respect. I have also become more explicitly aware of the emotional labour that our work generates, especially as GPs, where we deal with high levels of emotional and social distress on a daily basis, with no reliable safety mechanisms in place for the caregiver. Finding a language to articulate this has been invaluable, and as a leader, it has meant that I have championed change, to see substantive mechanisms put in place to recognise this, to help us navigate this, and support us to keep going.

To use the analogy of a good friend and colleague of mine:

> for people working in jobs that involve physical labour, there are required rules and safety nets that are non-negotiable. Without hard-hats and high-visibility clothing, you're simply not allowed on the building site. In jobs with recognised emotional labour, where are the safety nets? What is in place to protect us from the invisible psychological masonry that flies around our consulting rooms?

We need reflective practice, peer support, and self-care woven into the fabric of our working weeks if we are to protect ourselves, and our patients, from harm.

During this time, I also realised the importance of social activism in medicine. I learned from more experienced colleagues the value and importance of using our professional voice on behalf of those who had none and how this could translate into practical advocacy: meeting with local MSPs, inviting politicians and civil servants to visit our practice and witness work on the frontline, offering patients practical support to lobby for change, undertaking selective media work, raising formal questions in parliament. Not only did this help patients to feel heard, understood, and represented, but it also offered opportunities for collaborative working with voluntary sector colleagues, often 'hidden' from public view, under-recognised, undervalued, and unsustainably funded. An unexpected personal benefit of this social activism and advocacy work was protection from compassion fatigue and burnout. I found values congruence and a renewed sense of perspective and purpose, from refusing to accept the status quo, to using my professional influence to its best effect.

Advocacy was one of the founding principles of the Scottish Deep End project, a movement established in 2009, bringing together the GPs working in the 100 practices in Scotland serving the most socio-economically disadvantaged communities. It was inspired and informed by the work and principles of pioneering Welsh GP Dr Julian Tudor Hart, who first described the Inverse Care Law, and whom I had the enormous privilege of meeting, many years ago. At the end of my term with RCGP, I was asked to take on the role of chair of the Deep End group, with whom I had worked closely during that time. I accepted, with humility, gratitude, and hope. In the Deep End group, I had met inspiring, passionate, values-driven colleagues and had found a renewed sense of identity and purpose. I felt I had found my tribe, working alongside clinicians and academics in pursuit of health equity, with a focus on workforce, education, advocacy, and research. It was also an opportunity to continue much of the work that I had been involved with at a national level, especially during the Covid pandemic, which has shone a spotlight on pre-existing inequality, and, with that, a renewed focus on equitable recovery policy. The political stakes are high to ensure that recovery of services doesn't worsen things further. It is felt that there is a genuine interest and urgency in how we do things better as a country, from reducing the devasting number of drug deaths to improving vaccine uptake in our poorest communities, from improving access to mental health support to how we equip, train, support, and resource clinicians working on the frontline. Much of my time so far in this role has involved helping to shape and influence policy and strategy, presenting at meetings and conferences, recording podcasts, hosting roundtable discussions, and working alongside our professional organisations (the RCGP and the BMA) to help create the conditions for general practice teams to achieve their potential in addressing health inequalities.

I enjoy the 'bigger-picture' thinking and opportunity for change that leadership roles bring, but it has always felt important to me to remain grounded in my frontline clinical practice as a GP. Working within a deprived community informs and enriches both the context and the credibility of my work at a national level, but this has not been without its challenges. Working in dual roles require a significant personal investment of time and energy to do them well, and it can be difficult to make the 'brain switch' between the two. I have recognised that for me, there is a definite tipping point in clinical practice, where the job becomes harder if I am doing it less: harder to offer continuity of care to patients, harder to remain involved in decision-making in the practice, harder to keep up to date with our rapidly expanding generalist knowledge base, and harder to keep pace with the intensity of the work, when essential automatic decision-making abilities are impaired. The national leadership roles I have done have often demanded visibility, media presence, a flexible working week and high-level strategic thinking, often with little time for preparation. At several points over the years, I have felt that I have been constantly apologising to patients, colleagues, and family for trying to accommodate these competing demands. But perhaps what I really needed was to apologise to myself for the unrealistic expectations I have placed on myself. Meeting regularly with a professional coach, finding a language for the issue of 'cognitive overload' and putting mechanisms in place to ensure safe clinical practice, better communication with colleagues, and a more sustainable way of working have all helped, but it is work in progress.

What have my key insights been over the years? I have been extremely fortunate to have had positive role models and opportunity over the years. If I could advise my younger self, these are some of the things I would say to her:

- Choose work that aligns with your values. Doing hard stuff is so much easier when it does; the constant 'rub' of values incongruence can be exhausting and damaging. Say 'yes' to the things that you care about and interest you, rather than the things that others expect you to do.
- Build and invest in relationships with those inside and outside your organisation. Lasting change or improvement will not happen without them.

- Seek consensus where consensus is possible (and know when to compromise).
- Don't avoid conflict if there is no alternative, but be a kind, critical friend; if the existing relationships are respectful and healthy, the feedback will land better.
- First listen to understand, not to respond.
- Speak up: don't be afraid to offer a considered opinion, even if it doesn't conform.
- Try to present solutions rather than problems.
- Learn from your mistakes and failures, accept responsibility, and move on.
- Be self-aware: seek to understand how you align or conflict with others. Seek the views of those most different from you to learn the most. Recognise your own signs of stress and how that impacts on your behaviour and decision-making.
- Don't be afraid to be vulnerable and ask for help. It can be the most powerful thing you ever do.
- Sustain yourself as a leader. Invest in your team, learn to delegate, and decline well; consider coaching.
- Use your voice on behalf of those who have no voice.
- Use your training, your skills, your privilege, and your influence to leave the world in a better place than you found it.

Commentary

How often are we told that the problems we will tackle as leaders in the modern world will be complex in the sense of being unpredictable, unclear, and even insoluble? It isn't long before we can feel the texture of that complexity for ourselves; nothing seems straightforward, and things rarely go as planned. And the complexity that we become aware of is not just in the nature of external problems, but also in the volatility and uncertainty we feel within ourselves.

Carey, an effective leader at many levels of influence from her practice to the national stage, mirrors the vulnerability that so many of us feel. She describes how people rarely feel ambitious about taking on the mantle of leadership, how we don't feel ready before that opportunity arises and when we take it up, how little opportunity we have to prepare our response to the events that urgently clamour for our attention. It sounds distressing because it can be, but Carey has found a way of doing more than survive.

She has a rudder that keeps her moving in the right direction, and for her that rudder is the care she devotes to encouraging relationships to flourish.

How about you? What distressing or destabilising feelings do you suffer, especially when working with others as a teammate or leader? Is there something or someone that you use as a rudder, keeping you stable and on track?

In her journey, Carey describes how her experiences of problem-solving in the worlds of medicine and research were useful but not sufficient to tackle the issues she cared about most, especially the suffering of people with little power to help themselves. To address these, she needed collaboration from people who may not have seen that the issue was relevant, let alone important, to them. Her insight was that emotional intelligence, directed towards relationship-building, is fundamental to fostering that collaboration.

Emotional intelligence sounds like jargon. What meaning, if any, does it have for you? How have you developed your skills in this area? If you haven't, what is holding you back?

Let's develop this further with a couple of points. Firstly, emotional intelligence is the combination of emotional awareness and the intelligent analysis that we apply to it. For example, using our intelligence to go behind the feelings and behaviours that we become aware of in others, and ask *why* these occur and what the implications could be for how we move forward together.

Secondly, emotional intelligence needs to be applied to ourselves just as much as to others we interact with. In doing so, we switch repeatedly between the external and internal worlds, reflecting on our experiences, often in the moment so that we behave with greater understanding than we might otherwise have done.

How self-aware are you regarding your feelings and needs? Carey uses reflection and coaching to attend to her well-being; what approaches work for you?

If we seek collaboration, we need people to feel connected to us and what we collectively value. It helps to know, as Maya Angelou memorably said, that people may forget what we say and do, but they won't forget how we make them feel. There are many emotions that people may feel through interacting that foster a connection between us. These include feeling optimistic, resourceful, resilient, or especially, feeling the compassion that comes from sharing our vulnerabilities. At a deeper level, people develop a strong connection if they feel that we both care about them as people *and* care about what matters to them in their lives and why.

This insight can transform the way we approach people and situations. For example, think about when you are being opposed, say, in a meeting. What is your mindset at that point? Are you wanting to assert your point of view, or are you seeking to understand why the opposers feel as they do? Where would you usually be on that scale? Only you can hear your response, so be honest with yourself.

Carey illustrates how listening to understand, not just to influence, transforms situations in which we would previously have been trying to convert others. People see that we care enough to listen and explore, and this not only changes understanding but also changes attitudes on both sides. We can now see why what seems like a paradox is not a paradox at all; that is, the less that we try to influence, the more influence we actually have.

That may sound like an aphorism, a memorable soundbite, but it would be a shame to dismiss it as such. Listening to understand where someone is coming from is powerful because it is fundamental. Without it, we continue to operate from assumptions which are often unhelpful. It may not come easily because our biases and ways of thinking and behaving are well-worn, but it undoubtedly can be developed through practice, so give it a go and see what happens. We'd encourage you to be brave, maybe by being sufficiently open about how you are trying to overcome your ignorance or bias. This can really help to change the culture in a community in a way that could transform relationships.

As we relate better to each other, we open up about more significant things that might previously have been hidden from view. For instance, although it is said that people are resistant to change, what they are perhaps more afraid of is not change per se, but loss.

Listening is important, but it is not a passive process, and in seeking to understand, we also need to explore. When you are meeting resistance, do you try and find out what people are frightened about, particularly what they are frightened of losing? This may be money but may be other things that are just as significant to them like status, opportunities for advancement, or privileges. These potential losses are powerful blocks, and people often need help with disclosing or even discovering them for themselves. Time spent doing this can save so much anguish down the line.

As we can see, what previously might have been toxic encounters of confrontation and rigidity become journeys on which we learn more about each other, come to care about each other more, and find ourselves *wanting* to collaborate. We also learn more about what we have in common and what binds us. What we learn through dialogue may be incidental and unexpected, but it may be really significant, like finding our common purpose as Carey describes. Here we can be proactive because we can look out for what seems to jointly motivate us, and by discussing and clarifying it, we can help it to emerge and be strong.

Even when the issue that brought us to discussion seems no further forward because there is no resolution or concrete outcome, we should not see this as failure because the dialogue will have helped to build relationships, which is itself of great value. This isn't just confined to the human connections that people make with each other, but importantly includes the skills of working effectively together. People who forge links like this become a network that can assist each other by quickly coming together when situations arise, particularly urgent ones like the Covid pandemic.

'No man is an island', and significant issues that affect one community will have consequences for others; that's a fact that many with power, especially those who think tribally, are sometimes blind to. When building the arsenal of commitment and resource that are needed to address these issues, we have to show people how the issue affecting others may also affect them in ways that matter. For this we need to choose and use the language, data, and examples that resonate with them and have impact.

As these connections and implications are understood, a fire is lit, and as Carey shows, we can fan the flames through social activism, engaging the people and organisations that care and could have an influence. Whether those with power are motivated by self-interest more than by genuine care for others is perhaps less important than moving things forward.

People may not have to have 'acceptable' motives to do useful things. Do you agree with that or, if you feel uneasy, where does that feeling come from? Is there a risk that the conditions you place on someone's motives may compromise the good that they could do for the wider community?

As we've seen, to be effective is to collaborate, and the effort involved is sustained and deep because it requires us to care, which is not something we can switch on and off. Caring connects us to each other and to ourselves. It's a way of living and leading that brings meaning and purpose to those who choose that path. By showing how we matter to each other, it also brings hope to humanity.

As Carey shows, caring about people and relationships is the rudder that keeps us steady and pointed in the right direction through the choppy waters of our problems. Our job is to keep a strong hold on it.

Further reading from *The Leadership Hike*

Chapter 4 on using self-awareness to develop better connections with others.
Chapter 9 on how to converse better through listening better.
Chapter 19 on how to create consensus and how this is different from compromise.
Chapter 25 on how being ourselves helps to anchor us.

Podcast with the author

In this podcast, Carey Lunan discusses health inequality and transferrable skills including:

- The 'unworried unwell', why she is driven by health inequality, and how medical training left her unprepared to address this.
- Why relationship building is the key not only to helping patients but to helping the system to change at practice level and beyond.
- How skills gained through the consultation can be used to influence those with power such as politicians and policy makers.

CHAPTER

6

Darshna Patel

Darshna Patel is deputy head of workforce planning for the former Health Education England (now NHSE), former vaccine programme director for Kingsbury Mandir, and a GP pharmacist. She qualified as a pharmacist before moving into NHS management, and more recently she has specialised in workforce planning. Darshna was named as one of the 50 Leading Lights in the 2021 Kindness and Leadership Awards, partly in recognition of her work in setting up the world's first vaccination centre in a Hindu temple, the Kingsbury Mandir.

When considering leadership in the healthcare setting, it's worth appreciating that we aren't looking for Lord Sugar's next apprentice. And whilst, in the current populist climate, ruthlessly climbing the greasy pole to gain power and status might get us recognition, I think it's worth asking whether that's what we truly wish to be recognised and remembered for.

For me, leadership in any sector should be steeped in kindness – to those around us and to ourselves. And so, the questions I'm interested in exploring here are these:

1. What does it mean to lead with kindness?
2. How can we lead with kindness if it isn't endemic in the culture around us?

DOI: 10.1201/9781003270492-7

What does it mean to lead with kindness?

Kindness is often interpreted to be a sense of fluffy acts, or ways of being; 'be nice to everyone all the time' or 'treat others how you want to be treated'. However, for me, in its most genuine capacity, kindness is where treating others how *they* wish to be treated meets with valuing yourself and what you and those around you each bring to the table.

This concept recently came to life for me whilst I was co-leading a large PCN Covid vaccination centre based on the grounds of a Hindu temple. Running it called for a heady collaborative leadership approach. Within days, we'd brought together a large workforce whereby 200 people worked to deliver vaccinations each day. Within weeks, we were delivering 3200 vaccines a day. This was at times a leading rate in London. Diversity, collaboration, efficiency, and creativity were essential, and at the core was kindness. It's what brought us all together in the first place and the glue that held us together through the inevitable challenges.

Kindness was cultivated in one key way – proactively breaking down traditional hierarchies. Well-ingrained societal constructs mean that health services are often attributed to hard-working doctors and nurses. This is true. What is equally as true is that those same services would come apart at the seams without its porters, cleaners, administrators, managers, assistants, associates, healthcare scientists, allied health professionals, pharmacists, trainees, students, and a whole range of other clinical and non-clinical professionals. Challenging these hierarchies involves valuing the contribution of each individual equally, recognising that it's about levels of practice, the skills and 'tools' required to operate there, and crucially, that every level is a vital cog in a high-performing system. Vaccinating illustrates this perfectly.

Vaccines were delivered by those with the skills and ability to do so appropriately – clinicians and non-clinicians alike – regardless of their title, profession, or position in the unwritten hierarchy. It is all too easy to pay lip service to the idea that 'we're in it together', particularly in times of extreme pressure. For it to be *felt* in our vaccination centre, for it to be authentic, it was key that kindness permeated through our actions. Actions like challenging ourselves to deploy a fully diverse workforce of non-healthcare professionals, healthcare students/associates, and a range of non-clinical/clinical healthcare professionals – at times there was only one medic on site. And whilst this diversity was great, it also needed to be backed by equal pay for equal work (i.e., equivalent levels of autonomy and risk) – a level of fairness and transparency that, when done well, helped individuals feel valued and fostered trust. When deconstructing the traditional hierarchy, it needs to be done sensitively, carefully balancing the need to maintain professional and personal identity, and ensuring people feel valued by our actions and behaviours. Though I'm not suggesting we nailed it perfectly, I genuinely believe this authentic core value is what helped us create and nurture a true primary care network – care for the community delivered with and by the community.

There is a growing body of research which seems to show that performing acts of kindness can help refill our empty cups and build our resilience. This is certainly true for me. The privilege of being able to offer kindness and hope through vaccination during such a bleak period will stay with me for a lifetime. Through one of the biggest challenges in my career to date, both giving and receiving kindness is what kept me going. If I've learnt anything from this pandemic, it's that kindness comes into its own in times of crisis.

It is said that 'kindness doesn't cost anything'. I think I would probably want to caveat that as 'kindness *with healthy boundaries* doesn't cost anything'. Reflecting back, I'm beginning to understand the depth to which I gave both professionally and personally to achieve what we did. The more drained I felt, the more I gave to others, telling myself that 'acts of kindness will help refill my empty cup'. It strikes me now that those acts of kindness needed to be directed to *myself* as well. Though I had certainly not connected the dots in this way at the time, I see now that I was struggling to refill my cup because I wasn't being kind to myself. I wasn't holding some of my most fundamental boundaries, never mind the boundaries that help build resilience. And as trite as this may sound, we genuinely cannot be the effective leaders the world really needs, now more than ever, without being kind to ourselves too.

This is still very much a work in progress for me, a tough daily practice. As with anything, I can only share what this looks like from where I currently am on this journey. I have started reflecting more deeply around what and where my boundaries are, and where I need them to be – the power of 'why' has been a great tool to unshroud what lurks beneath the surface. Suffice to say this is not always comfortable and takes energy in and of itself, but the allure of discovery keeps drawing me in. I'm also trying to build the muscle to be okay with not being okay.

Alongside that, I'm starting to embrace how empowering it feels to use accountability, instead of shame, to hold both myself and others accountable, and by virtue, have healthier boundaries. I thought I understood what this meant, and was doing it, because it's Leadership 101, right? But that couldn't have been further from the truth. True accountability is much more nuanced and takes real effort and energy. Brené Brown's podcasts have been instrumental in unlocking this relatively new exploration for me. It may resonate with you, that you know what you should be doing to be kind to yourself as a leader but struggle to follow through with consistent action. If it does, I wholeheartedly recommend diving into some of Brené's work, or another exploration of your own. After all, curiosity is not just a vital asset for leadership; it's a superpower.

How can we lead with kindness if it isn't endemic in the culture around us?

Where to start with this? Well, for one, it's recognising that you don't have to be in a formal leadership position to do this, but either way, it's tough stuff. This is hard because it involves going against the grain, it involves doing something new and different and brave. First things first, we need to be upfront with ourselves about this. On one level, there is an internal urge to do it, and on another level, a conscious awareness. When they come together, there emerges an *acceptance* of the possible consequences.

Leading with kindness where that isn't the endemic culture challenges the status quo. It involves putting your head above the parapet. Sometimes, this comes with minimal personal risk, for example with the hidden, less visible, day-to-day acts of kindness. Sometimes, however, the stakes are much higher. We need only consider whistleblowing to remind ourselves that those who choose to lead in this way sometimes put it all on the line, from their career and livelihood to their health and well-being.

To help find solace through what can be incredibly challenging, it is important to first understand the potential implications and *honestly* consider whether or not we would be okay if things do pan out that way. What we need in these moments is for the place where the power, privilege, and resource lie to *also* take on the responsibility – a problem shared is a problem halved. Sometimes, though, this doesn't happen. It's in those times, and in times when we've tried but things aren't turning out as we'd hoped, that this concept of *shared responsibility* can help us find peace in inaction or perceived failure. It is equally important to work on becoming more comfortable with uncertainty and holding any inevitable tension, learning to sit with paradox, embracing the 'and' between competing ideas or truths. As I said, this isn't easy stuff, but (*and*) the rewards are that much sweeter.

Where I saw this modelled

Some years ago, I worked in hospital land. I recall a point in time where I found myself having to navigate a myriad of complex ethical dilemmas – ones that would still challenge most. I was a relatively junior pharmacist, trying to carry the weight of systemic challenges, and it felt like I was doing it alone. Exasperated and exhausted, I shared this, without intention, with a ward matron. I found unexpected kindness in my conversation with her. It was unexpected not just because, in my mind, I hadn't asked for or done anything to deserve it, but also because it bucked against the culture, or at least my experience of it.

In a moment of vulnerability which challenged my core values, when I didn't know where to turn professionally, she recognised that in me and listened. This wasn't about giving me answers; it was about validating concerns which weren't validated before and giving me tools to find the answers for the person I was. The dynamics of that working environment meant that we would never really have had that conversation. It was of no benefit to her but had huge implications for me. I'm grateful because that rare gem of kindness allowed me not to compromise who I am when I was most vulnerable. Thank you, Clare.

How I pay it forward

1. ***Making ripples:*** Most of the time, we aren't in a position to make huge waves, especially when the tide is against us. Though it sounds like a tautology, leading with kindness when it isn't experienced is hard and often starts with the small things. For me, that has usually meant finding the courage to speak out and challenge traditional thinking around hierarchies and power. At present, I am consciously trying to avoid shaming (self and others) and trying to step in to not allow shaming where I bear witness. Individually, these are small ripples, but I do them with the awareness that my contribution matters. The tragedy of the pandemic is a great example. It has created opportunities for countless ripples of kindness – ripples which over time become waves that can shift the cultural tide.
2. ***Nurturing psychological safety:*** Psychological safety is more than a buzzword or a box to be ticked. We need to talk about it, temperature test it, and agree to value and to maintain it. Creating psychological safety in teams where we can is desirable at the best of times and essential in today's world. For me, this means creating spaces to really connect with people – to let each other be truly seen and heard. We need to feel safe enough to be vulnerable and honest so that we can support our individual and collective resilience. No matter our job title, banding, or level of organisation-wide influence, we can work to create micro-havens in our teams and grow kindness from the ground up.
3. ***Being authentically kind:*** This is difficult and a daily practice for me. But kindness coming from a place of authenticity is so powerful. If we think about it, I'm sure we can all recall a time where we've

experienced inauthentic kindness. We may not register it consciously but are often aware that something doesn't feel quite right. When kindness comes from a genuine place that is true to us, our words, body language, and actions are automatically congruent. This builds trust and demonstrates the art of the possible. After all, there is nothing more powerful than being the change you want to see.

Kindness is contagious – you catch it like the flu

We cannot fight for kindness unless we experience it. But when we do, you can be sure that kindness breeds kindness. I firmly believe the success of our vaccination centre was underpinned by collaboration, a collective mission to do good, and a kind of viral kindness. Volunteers giving up their valuable time to support strangers, donation of the incredible site, provision of free lunch (and a bean-to-cup coffee machine), paid work for those who'd lost their jobs, and so many more kind acts were all part of bringing hope to communities during one of humanity's greatest hours of need. Every act of kindness was contagious. We saw how, given the right conditions, kindness can go viral. Seeing that health and social care today increasingly require us to work with and across teams and organisations – just imagine how impactful viral kindness could be.

The three kindness keys of leadership

Develop behaviours to lead in the Social Age

Kindness is a crucial ingredient of collaborative leadership and collaboration is at the heart of leadership fit for the Social Age. It is what helps drive innovation at scale in today's modern world. Kindness is what allows us to create safe spaces to be vulnerable, to challenge and be challenged, to think differently, speak up, and to nurture our resilience. Kindness fosters trust, which in turn cultivates psychological safety – true collaboration cannot exist without this.

As primary care and healthcare as a whole evolves, it is clear the future is not about traditional professional hierarchies – every skill set adds value. Diversity is not simply desirable but critical to thrive, just as it is in nature. The introduction of Additional roles reimbursement scheme (ARRS) roles in general practice across England is a testament to this.

If we want to develop leadership behaviours (not tick-box skills) fit for the Social Age, we need to become adept and be comfortable navigating both 'old power' (i.e., traditional hierarchical leadership structures) and 'new power' (i.e., informal leadership and influence which often exists in the absence of a formal title or authority). We need to delicately balance the need to maintain professional and personal identity whilst avoiding pigeon-holing and (inter- and intra-)professional tribalism. We need to start to feel secure enough in ourselves to be able to truly see, hear, and collaborate with those around us, irrespective of positional power or age-old boundaries and barriers.

Equally, we cannot use (faux) collaboration as a guise to avoid making the difficult decisions – it is not a pass to choosing comfort over courage. There will be times when we need to make decisions which aren't about promoting collaboration; for example, not giving someone a pay rise or, in the case of our vaccination centre, making 'command and control' type decisions around people flow and personnel. These can often feel unkind. Utilitarian principles can help guide these and reframe our thinking around how kind or otherwise they are. Values-guided decisions, and transparency and expediency in communicating these can help make them both more palatable to be on the receiving end of and easier to live with. Ultimately, though, to be effective leaders who can lead across the piece, we must be able to sit more comfortably in paradoxes and work to master the fine art of *acknowledging* and holding the tension.

Think 'people' not 'resources'

If each person is a unique spice in the soup that is our NHS workforce, be the chef that cultivates the blend, be the dinner guest that embraces the individual flavours *and* the heady mix.

While head chef is a vital role, being a leader is not only about leading from the front and taking people with you. It is just as vital to lead from within and be the dinner guest that speaks passionately and honestly about how the complex mix of spices lifts the entire dish. Be the one that encourages others to be brave and try this contemporary cuisine.

Recognising that we are greater than the sum of our parts, and what one person brings to the table can be enhanced by another, is the crux of leading with kindness. It is about valuing each individual and fostering collaboration to create something even better. And for clarity, collaboration is not the opposite of leadership – both can and need to co-exist. The ability to lead, collaborate, *and* do both at the same time, depending on the situation, doesn't just empower people; it inspires them.

Be kind to you, too

We cannot lead effectively unless we look after ourselves too. This doesn't necessarily mean that we put our own oxygen mask on first, as is generally espoused in leadership chatter. Life can sometimes be too complex and messy to do that in a clearly defined way. Perhaps it's sometimes enough to put our mask on *as well* and do a bit of both whilst staying receptive to how we are feeling and not ignoring our early warning signs.

As well as the oxygen mask, we need the life jacket that is our support network. We need to surround ourselves with people we can connect and be vulnerable with to create spaces where we experience and grow kindness. It is key to be able to recharge and refill the cup in a guard down, mask down, connected way. Similarly, we don't always have to have the answers to everything. It's okay to say we don't know and to surround ourselves with a network of colleagues and friends, within and outside of healthcare, to soundboard issues and discuss options. I really value the fresh perspective that I get from those who work in completely different fields and the kindness that they lead with when they offer me that support. Beyond that, I couldn't do most of what I do without them – thank you, Sonal, Vani, and Jaz for being the life jackets I've so desperately needed of late.

Finally, and perhaps most importantly, *kindness is not finite*. It's not cake. If I take a bigger slice, it doesn't mean you'll end up with a smaller one. We can be kind to others and kind to ourselves too without depleting the kindness reserves; *kindness is viral, it multiplies and grows*. By being kind to ourselves, we create space and capacity to be kind to others. As leaders in healthcare, I think this is possibly one of the hardest and kindest things we can do for ourselves, our colleagues, and our patients.

Commentary

Darshna's experiences provoked us to think more deeply about kindness and its role in the workplace, particularly from leaders. Kindness feels like something more than valuing people and their contribution. Collins defines kindness as *the quality of being gentle, caring, and helpful*, and this really resonates with us, because of the emphasis on gentleness. The kindest acts are those carried out in the moment and with no fanfare. Being kind requires us to consider what someone else might be feeling and choose a response that takes either their short-term or long-term well-being into account. Kindness is the extra cup of tea presented quietly on your desk by a team member who recognises you are having a bad day. Kind teams send 'get well soon' wishes to a colleague who is unwell, even though this means they will all be working harder. A kind leader might tell a member of staff it is fine to leave early to cope with a family crisis with no consequence to pay or future hours.

Think about your own workplace. What are the small acts of kindness you witness? Is there any pattern you notice about who are the givers and receivers of kindness and the impact this has on how the organisation feels and functions?

The benefits are clear. Working in an environment where people perform kind acts makes us feel both valued and safe and gives us a greater sense of belonging to the organisation. This helps us perform well, and we are more likely to stay in our jobs. When people who work in healthcare feel safe, they are more likely to speak up when they notice something amiss, meaning our patients are safer too.

Psychological and neuroscientific studies over decades have shown the benefits on the 'doer' of the kind act. A single act of kindness can result in the release of endorphins and oxytocin which generate a feeling of well-being and create new neural connections. The new connections make it easier to think and act kindly in future.

Experiencing (giving, receiving, or witnessing) kind acts at work both reflects and influences the culture of the organisation itself. Culture is often the most important factor in the success of the organisation, so it's good for leaders to have an awareness of factors which might be barriers to team members expressing kindness towards each other (and towards patients), as kindness seems to be something that connects us to our very humanity. We lose connection to this at our peril.

Think about the barriers people may face to expressing kindness towards patients and work colleagues. Do you recognise that you also face barriers or dilemmas when trying to choose the kindest response to a situation?

There are many facets to kindness. Sometimes when we consider another person's difficulties, we make some assumptions about what the impact may be on them and act in what we intend to be a kind way to mitigate this. If this assumption is wrong, then the act of kindness may be seen to be an act of judgement and we can be in danger of coming across as patronising and condescending. This can be accentuated by the power imbalance that may exist due to our leadership role, or professional status. Power imbalance can get in the way of both how our acts of kindness are received, and how we receive the kindness of others.

Have you ever felt irritated when someone apologises to you for something that you felt didn't warrant an apology? In apologising we usually assume that our action or omission has been to the detriment of someone else, and if they don't perceive this in the same way, the apology itself can be a cause of consternation and even generate a feeling of guilt in the receiver of the apology. Acts of kindness can sometimes misfire in a similar way.

In a context where you are a leader, your acts of kindness may be closely observed by others who are checking for fairness. This may be an issue if some members of the team have, for example, more challenging home lives than others and so need more acts of kindness and understanding when this impacts their work. In an organisational culture where it is normal for people to share their difficulties and to help each other, it will be easier for leaders to show kindness openly without fear of being accused of bias. In a similar way, leaders might observe kind acts between certain team members, but with the needs of others being ignored, and this might be an indication that cliques or subcultures are at play in the organisation.

In another scenario, an act of kindness might be seen as an attempt to manipulate a situation, for the sake of a later gain for yourself. This is more likely if your organisational culture has become too 'transactional', where work gets done based on performance-related rewards or sanctions and where relationships are less highly valued. In UK primary care, the drive to greater efficiency and the contracting systems can encourage this. It may mean your simple act of kindness is not recognised for what it is – one human being reaching out to another to soothe at a difficult time. Authentic kindness is something that comes from the heart, not the head, overrides power, is non-judgemental, and is something we offer without expectation of a 'return on investment'.

Think about how you receive kindness when offered by team members. Do you ever perceive this as an attempt to manipulate you or to pass judgement on your ability to cope with challenge? Does this vary depending on who is showing kindness or how you are feeling about yourself at the time?

Some people find it difficult to receive kindness, as they may interpret your act as meaning you don't believe they have the resilience or strategies to cope with the challenging situation. They may have been socialised through life to believe accepting help from others is a demonstration of weakness and therefore your kindness may be hard for them to bear, and you will find it 'thrown back in your face'. In these situations, your act of kindness may cause distress to both the recipient and to you.

Has your own act of kindness ever backfired or not been received as you hoped? Why might that have been?

The need for kindness recognises our human vulnerability. People, particularly leaders, are not always at ease with their vulnerability and struggle when they know it has been noticed by others. In her book *Daring Greatly*, Brené Brown suggests vulnerability can be 'the birthplace of love, belonging, joy, courage, empathy, and creativity'. If we embrace our vulnerability and learn to share this, letting our team know when we might be feeling uncertain or overwhelmed, we also give them permission to show their kindness without fear it will be badly received. We can then further develop the culture of kindness by noticing kind acts, acknowledging them, and being grateful. Remembering how much the giver benefits from the act of kindness, showing our vulnerability becomes an opportunity for others to thrive.

So, giving and receiving kindness can be a complex area. Darshna feels kindness is 'where treating others how they wish to be treated meets with valuing yourself and what you and those around you each bring to the table'. It takes skill to do this and involves knowing both when an act of kindness is needed and when it might be welcomed. The first includes developing your radar to spot suffering/distress or potential suffering. Our ability to spot suffering will depend on many variables and will vary with how distracted we are by our own lives and difficulties. Those living with a neurodivergent condition such as autism or ADHD might find this more difficult, particularly when, in a work environment, colleagues often hide how they feel. Alternatively, there are some who spot the potential for suffering too readily because they base their conclusion on how they might feel in the same circumstance. The better we know each other at work, the more likely we are to pick up clues, such as changes in usual behaviour and responses, which might indicate some special care, and acts of kindness might be needed. Remember it is the quiet, gentle acts that can have the greatest impact as they support without throwing people off balance and without taking away their sense of control of the situation. Then watch for the clues that your kindness has landed well. In primary care consulting we call this their 'acceptance set'. If the kind act is rejected, you may have misinterpreted the situation, or they may not yet feel comfortable sharing their vulnerability.

Darshna completes her reflections with emphasis on our need to be kind to ourselves. Just with others, this will mean a certain amount of anticipation of our needs and self-forgiveness when, due to distractions or stress, we are unable to perform the kind acts we know will be good for others and for ourselves.

Maybe kindness is at its best when it is spontaneous, authentic, and with no power issues – maybe anonymously given, and given with sensitivity to how it might be received.

Further reading from *The Leadership Hike*

Chapters 8 and 9 for how to communicate, particularly using effective listening.

Chapter 16 for more on how to be kind to yourself, particularly in adverse circumstances.

Chapter 18 on how to encourage the contributions of others.

Podcast with the author

In this podcast, Darshna Patel shares her journey from hospital pharmacist to her current role at NHSE and talks about:

- What it means to lead with kindness.
- The importance of being kind to yourself.
- How to stay kind, even when the performance of a team member isn't what you had hoped for.
- The importance of 'power-sharing'.

CHAPTER

7

Ben Allen

Dr Ben Allen has been a GP partner at Birley Health Centre since 2018. During the first few years of this role, he focused his leadership on the task of developing a highly performing team at his GP practice. Having used this experience as a springboard to learning more about leadership, he took on a role in commissioning and more recently as clinical director for primary care in Sheffield, in the South Yorkshire Integrated Care System (ICS). His main interests include empowering patients to understand their health and the health system and building high-performing teams with high morale, confidence, and autonomy.

I hated my first 7 years a doctor. Eventually, the clinical confidence came.

The following year, a developed a love of quality improvement which was quickly followed by leadership.

I've loved my last 5 years. Here is some of my story.

In my final year as a GP trainee, I eventually felt I had the knowledge and confidence to manage the complex job of being a GP. After a further year of locuming I became a GP partner. We had lots of the ingredients needed for a great practice: well-staffed with excellent GPs, a stable practice population, and a great building. However, patient satisfaction was much lower than expected. There was a sense that low satisfaction was a result of funding not keeping pace with demand, which was true. However, what was *also* true is that things were not working as well as they could be. The cumulative result of all our missed opportunities was causing avoidable impact on our patients and also our staff. As someone responsible for the service, I felt quite distressed with this situation.

DOI: 10.1201/ 9781003270492-8

This situation reminded me of cycling. Have you ever ridden a bike that hasn't been well maintained? The gears don't change, it rattles, it brakes slowly, and one tyre is almost flat. It really slows you down, but *also* it is disheartening to ride. You know it has good components; it has potential. If it were more finely tuned, it could be a pleasure to ride with less effort. But if you're cycling from one emergency to the next, always behind schedule, there is no time for maintenance. One of my early roles at our surgery was just to notice if something like this was happening. But even if you *have* noticed it, the skills needed for maintenance are not the same as the riding you've been practicing.

The first thing I did was smart. The second thing wasn't. I felt to get a perspective on the problems I would speak, in person, to every staff member. I asked what motivates them, what makes them feel valued, and what challenges we were facing. The main challenges at the time were communication, patient access, team working, and consistency. We knew what the problems were. What we didn't know was how to solve them.

My early attempts to make improvements involved *me* trying to improve problems that were actually symptoms of deeper cultural problems. For example, trying to create systems for blood test results and medication reviews, or dealing with staff issues by trying to create fairness. But basically, they had limited impact or I could not do it.

So, I started to learn. I read and watched videos on organisational development and leadership, by authors like Simon Sinek, Jim Collins, Patrick Lencioni, Brené Brown, and Nancy Kline. There were overlapping themes, but I was able to create a framework that included all the principles. The three main areas were nurturing potential in the team, team dynamics, and being purpose and values driven.

Given that the resources coming into the NHS are likely to be fairly static, the main opportunity for improvement is releasing the full potential in our team. It is also about creating an environment where people love coming to work which, as a leader, just seems the right thing to do. These values were already present; however, it was the application that was incomplete. So how did we release potential?

Everyone needs someone in the organisation who knows them, professionally and personally, who cares about them, who can help them play to their strength, overcome challenges, develop, and challenge to grow. It is not possible to do this well for more than around ten people. So we needed a structure of team leaders to do this. However, we also needed to ensure that those team leaders had the natural strengths to fulfil this role.

One way to find who is natural at this is to ask the staff who are already doing this for them. Leadership roles often find their way to people who are clinically senior and of higher social status, people who are confident and charismatic. Often the best people to lead teams will not be obvious to you. It may be even less obvious to themselves. They need finding and encouraging. Questions answered by the staff – such as 'Who do you admire?' – were an excellent guide. We had to do some careful rearranging of roles to get the right people leading the teams. This is difficult to do, but once achieved, teams self-organise, thrive, and continually improve by themselves.

One of the early principles was the importance of recruitment. With a friend who works in recruitment, and an excellent book called *Who* by Geoff Smart, I set about learning how to do great recruitment in my own time. We had an extraordinarily high turnover of reception staff, so this was a chance to learn. The main principles were finding people with the right character and values (skills can be taught): a person's past predicts their future, and *you can't spend too long on recruitment.* Our reception team now are on another level. When the time came to needing a manager, I initially felt uncomfortable spending so much of my time on recruitment. Now, everyone agrees it was all worth every minute.

In large organisations, board meetings would involve all the heads of departments. I noticed in GP surgeries, the partners meetings were made up of GPs plus a manager. So, in effect, most of the board was from one department. This meant that we lacked the views and perspectives we needed to understand the problems and make good decisions. When we created a new weekly meeting with the heads of department, we found we could deal with operational challenges more quickly and effectively. We also now have a 10-minute morning meeting with people from each department.

Another way to describe the processes above was Jim Collins' principle of 'getting the right people on the bus, the wrong people off the bus, and everyone in the right seats'. Getting the 'wrong people off the bus' can play out more compassionately than it sounds. It starts with ensuring there is relationship and trust built, so challenges can be made when needed. Most people respond well to this. Occasionally, there are people whose values or careers don't align with the organisation. Coming to this realisation together can be positive and kind for both.

The work on team dynamics comes from Patrick Lencioni's *The Five Dysfunctions of a Team.* The first and most important principle is to build vulnerability-based trust, or psychological safety. This is about creating a sense that it is safe to be honest and vulnerable. People need to know they can speak up about their weaknesses and challenges or problems in the organisation without any personal risk. This can be built by modelling it, celebrating when others are vulnerable, and *never* punishing it. Meetings can be facilitated to increase safety, for example allowing people to discuss in small groups and feedback together. Any exercise that stretches people to be a bit more vulnerable, if positive, also helps.

My favourite meeting was when our manager asked everyone to bring in three objects that were meaningful to them. As we went around, people explained what they had brought and why. Starting to talk about something you've brought is slightly easier than talking about yourself. We learned what matters to each other, about people's families, hobbies, and ultimately, about who they are as people. There was risk, vulnerability, tears, and lots of laughter. The team may have felt this was a nice break from the work. However in many ways, that was the most important work they did all day. Building trust is the foundation for great teamwork and is a high priority.

As trust develops, so does the team's ability to have honest and collaborative discussions about challenges. When this happens, we are all more likely to be committed to the decisions that are agreed. We may also be more likely to be able to hold each other to account about the decision.

Improvement work and leadership is often not as valued as clinical work. The results can take time to develop and can be harder to see. Initially, I did it in all in my own time. Over time, the results were becoming clearer, so I made a case for having paid time for the work. Thankfully my partners have been very supportive and agreed.

If I think about pivotal moments in my leadership journey, one was Covid. There was a need to create safety, dialogue, support, and encourage rapid adaption. Steps up in leadership are often done sensitively and carefully. However, the sense of urgency compelled me to take a lead in a way I had not previously done. Probably, it had been an open door for a while. Sometimes the need is what compels us to put our fears aside and 'push'.

I had an experience in a restaurant that taught me something about general practice. There was a long queue, and it was very busy. The team was working like clockwork. They knew every reservation and every order. Deep in concentration, unflustered, efficient, communicating with each other, they zipped about. Everything happened as it should. The staff seemed to have a deep sense of peace and satisfaction *despite the queue*. They seemed to draw their peace from the fact they were performing optimally and beautifully as a team. Their team identity was in their performance, not the queue.

In general practice, if a sense of peace and satisfaction is only attained when we meet demand, it will do us harm. It's not in our control. When we work in places that don't value or nurture staff, or with processes that waste effort and frustrate patients and staff, it will also do us harm. Changing that *is* possible. When we work in ways that feel increasingly effective, efficient, caring, and responsive, with systems and people working towards their full potential, there's a peace and satisfaction that comes from that. Demand is not in our control. Finding ways to enable a high performing team *is*.

After 5 years as a GP partner, I started using some of my time on GP leadership in Sheffield. I knew by now I enjoyed leadership and making an impact. A role came up on the 'governing body' at the Clinical Commissioning Group, and I wondered if working in an organisation with a leadership role would be a good fit. I soon learned governance wasn't the way I was going to make an impact. A role came up to lead several GP surgeries. I ignored it as the role felt beyond me. However, someone approached me to ask if I would apply. It was this that gave me the confidence to consider it and realise it was an excellent fit for what I enjoy. The end result was I actually gained a different role, as clinical director for primary care in Sheffield, which was also someone else's idea. Clearly, we need others to recognise our potential.

Leadership as a partner is hands-on, with authority to make changes. In my current role, I have some say in creating change to primary care across Sheffield. However, the real impact, I think, is in the culture of the teams in GP surgeries. So, the new challenge became how to influence change bottom up, by connecting with people who are doing the work. One barrier to this is the lack of a shared understanding that culture matters enough to prioritise. People need to be released by employers and have the time, headspace, and authority to make changes.

As I reflect on how well my current roles are suiting me, I am thinking about my values, strengths, and experience. I value rich relationships, authenticity, and making a positive difference. For my strengths, for which I also asked other people, I have thinking differently and compassionate leadership. My experience is clinical and building teams.

Any roles I get need to be balanced. I could take a role which offers the largest impact. But if it does not match my strength and certainly my values, it won't be a satisfying role.

So I can now ask the question, to what extent does the way I spend my time reflect who I am? It feels important that as individuals we are working in a way that honours who we are. I think the world would be all the better for it too. I'm aware there is progress I need to make on this.

Academic knowledge is often the ingredient for success. I think our social connections are going to play an increasing role. The mechanisms for gaining knowledge and opportunities may increasingly come through social networks. For me, 'X' (formerly Twitter) has been a significant part of my journey. It has been a place to learn from others, challenge thinking, exchange ideas, build relationships, and create opportunities.

Being coached has helped me on my journey too. I often find myself with a tangle of thoughts and feelings. Someone who is good at listening and asking questions can help me to unravel my thoughts, help me to prioritise, and hold me to account.

Overall, the last 5 years have been a joy. I've grappling with the most complex challenges I've ever come across, helping others to thrive, connecting with hundreds of people on Twitter, finding new roles that fit my strengths whilst on the whole, I maintained a reasonable balance with my life outside of work. I've tried to honour my values of developing trusted relationships, being authentic even when that requires courage and making a positive difference. I've tried to keep curious, nurtured potential and led with compassion. The beauty is you will have your own unique combination of values and strengths. If not already, I encourage you to discover and live whatever they are for you.

Commentary

We feel Ben's piece will resonate strongly with people who are relatively new to primary care leadership. He tells a story of someone who realised during the early part of his career that he needed more than day-to-day clinical work to be able to find joy at work; he needed to feel the service provided by the practice was delivering what the patients needed. We are driven to leadership for many reasons, and for many, the frustration of seeing how things could be is the main driving force. But for Ben it was more than mere frustration – it was the emotional impact, what he describes as *distress.* Instead of overriding this emotional awareness, he decided to try to put it to good use. He became the person who noticed both when things weren't going well and issues with systems and processes. Whilst having this 'permission' was a powerful gift, without the power to influence and enact change it can also feel like a burden.

Can you remember a time you noticed something at work that generated a strong emotional response? Was there an opportunity to turn this response into positive change, and if not, how could circumstances be changed to provide this opportunity?

Ben uses an analogy of the practice operating like a poorly maintained bike. He wisely recognised that conversations with each of the practice team members would be vital to understand the inner workings of the practice (or the bike), and it is likely that people feeling they had been listened to was an essential component of the change which later occurred.

His description of his early improvement attempts provides a useful lesson for all of us. His conversations with the team revealed to him where people felt the problems were with systems and processes, and he took this on board, taking on the task of improving the systems himself. It must have felt very disappointing that his efforts didn't make the difference he had hoped for.

Think about the last issue you tried to sort out at work. How did it go, and what factors do you feel contributed to either the success or failure?

What he later realised was the organisation may be able to fix itself, if only the people within it felt empowered to do so. Attempts leaders make to fix things themselves, no matter how well intentioned, may be the thing that is holding others back from being part of the solution. If leaders believe they have the best understanding of a problem, and the best idea to fix it, then teams may come to believe this, too, so why would they need to contribute? He highlights this also in his description of partners meetings. It is more likely that a group of people from the same professional group will think in a similar way, and this will limit the range of views and potential solutions. Diversifying the group can mitigate this and avoid groupthink.

Experts have studied leadership and management techniques for decades, so when Ben concluded that his first attempts to improve processes hadn't worked, he turned to the writings of these experts to see what he might draw from them. It takes humility to recognise others may be able to offer us guidance, and clearly Ben found the writing helpful.

Consider how you like to learn. Do you watch others in action, or do you prefer reading about the experiences of experts? Does social media play a role in your learning? If so, how do you do this safely without risking your well-being?

He gives practical tips on how he applied what he had learned to influence practice culture and develop a highly performing team. This is akin to ensuring you have a well-maintained bike before you ride, or a sharp saw before you start to cut wood. This is a wonderful description of how a leader can set up the right environment for others to flourish. He focused his leadership efforts on ensuring the right people were on board, that they had a functioning structure of 'mini-teams', that there was diversity of views and that other leaders were developed and supported. People feeling comfortable with each other seemed important in the development of trust, and Ben describes activities designed with this in mind. Trust within teams increases the sense of connection people feel to each other and commitment to the goals of the organisation.

Encouraging others to lead is not always as straightforward as it may seem. If individuals had been used to being 'led', this can be a hard habit to break; they need to feel they have 'permission' to take the initiative. In Ben's piece he describes how to choose the right people to lead the mini-teams, based on how they are perceived by the other staff. It's worth considering what it is about the person that is admired (e.g., pushing things through, standing up for something, relating well to people, being compassionate, going the extra mile). An awareness of this helps to match people to the right team. The next step is encouraging them to further develop the skills they will need, particularly active listening, problem-solving, and effective delegation. They are likely to have been spotted as they were already demonstrating this, but at times, once given a formal leadership role, some individuals feel they are supposed to suddenly 'be the boss' and know the answers, and so stop listening. Leaders developing other leaders can mitigate this by reinforcing the skills and attributes that led them to their position in the first place and encourage them to invest in building relationships, encouraging learning and peer support.

Think about where you work, and the teams that operate from the organisation. Do all team members act as if they can enact change where needed, or do they await the actions of the leaders? What do you witness that tells you whether there is trust or not? What can you do to influence this?

It is clear to see how much Ben has learned, and the satisfaction he has felt, in making a difference at his practice level. As well as learning how to develop his team, he developed insights into his own strengths as a leader – not only the things he is good at, but also the things that energise him. Having been encouraged by others to expand his role to the wider health service, he now reflects on which type of role fits his strengths most closely. It is when we are in a role that matches our strengths and values most closely that we do the most good.

If you are being encouraged to take on a leadership role in the wider system, what factors do you use to decide if this is the right path for you? How well do you understand yourself and what you value? Whilst new opportunities provide a chance to learn something new, they can also pull us away from the things we value.

We were struck in Ben's piece by his ability to take a 'balcony view' of his leadership. He was implementing change, and at the same time observing what was happening and reflecting, whilst applying tips and learning he picked up from books, conversations, and social media. Though it is likely he made some mistakes on the way, as we all do, this seemed to protect him from having to learn the hard way.

When thinking about your own leadership development, when might it be worth actively seeking out learning from the experience of others – by reading, by courses, by connecting on social media? How can you develop a 'balcony view' of your day-to-day work?

Further reading from *The Leadership Hike*

Chapter 5 on understanding yourself and playing to your strengths.
Chapter 9 on the art of a good conversation – how to use effective dialogue to empower others.
Chapter 11 on helping people to grow, especially building more leaders within your team.
Chapters 13 and 15 on becoming a team and leading the team to their best performance.

Podcast with the author

In this podcast, Ben Allen discusses the difference between leading at a practice level and a system level and the power of learning from the experience of others, including:

- How to develop a highly performing team using the distributed leadership model.
- The importance of building psychological safety in an organisation and how this can be achieved.
- The difference between leading at a practice level and a system level.
- The power of learning from the experience of others.

CHAPTER

8

Tracey Vell

Dr Tracey Vell worked in general practice for 27 years and for the NHS for 30 years. She has been involved in LMC leadership, educational leadership, and business start-ups across her years in practice.

She succeeded in bringing primary care providers to the Greater Manchester Health and Social Care Devolution programme and has worked as executive medical director for primary care for the GM health and social care partnership for over 6 years. More recently she has taken on the role of medical director for Health Innovation Manchester to spread innovation across health and care settings.

She supports, advises, and works amongst GPs and is passionate about the need for frontline providers to direct strategy with an approach that tackles wider determinants of health.

She was awarded an MBE in the New Year Honours in 2018 for her work.

Writing this piece gives me the opportunity in my journey to stand and observe the landscape looking both backwards and forwards. For me this is a scary proposition, as prolonged reflection and writing are the two areas I enjoy least.

For me, the past seems less visible and energising, especially when forward views contain so much passion and opportunity. Despite this I have enjoyed my meander through the leafy and at times lonely memories to return to areas of sunshine and clarity of purpose. In my leadership, I hope to have left enough of a path for others to see the way or at least where the going was treacherous and I turned back, enough of a warning not to travel.

DOI: 10.1201/9781003270492-9

A beginner leader

My earliest venture into leadership was as an SHO, first year out of house jobs. I decided to put up my hand to be junior doctor representative, mainly as no one else wanted to. I was naïve, young, and fresh, and this turned out to be the start of a bitter learning curve which shaped my personal leadership vision. On a visit by dignitaries to the hospital I was asked questions about my own experience of a 6-month post. I chose to respond honestly, and as a result I came under scrutiny with the result that my 6-month post was not recognised towards my general practice training, as the consultant would not sign off my experience.

As a young doctor I realised, for the first time, my small voice seemed not to matter to anyone in power. It was a surprise working within a supposedly caring profession to discover how anonymous one can feel. I remember that support seemed to move further away from me and be inaccessible, leaving me with feelings of doubt and misgivings. However, the sheer injustice and the need for others to not experience this and subsequent anxieties that I had felt spurred me on. My GP tutor offered no support, and I realised I was drowning in an unfamiliar environment. It was then that I met someone in regional leadership who gave me hope that the small voice can be heard and truth could win out. She believed in me and represented me nationally, succeeding in not just overturning the decision but in starting a fuller investigation into that department. Now, looking back at that point in my journey, I can see how it led to my decision to take a lead in the area of inclusivity and support.

On moving into my training practice and into a period of mentorship, my next landscape unfolded. My trainer was enthusiastic and had ideas and opinions that opened my mind to other areas of leadership beyond the clinical domain. He introduced me in 1994 to the local medical committee (LMC) as a registrar representative, and I have been associated with this organisation ever since. During this period I watched and learned. I saw how leadership was needed to support our sector (general practice) which was so fragmented, and as a result had a much weaker voice. I began to understand the feelings involved such as the passion and the need to fight, but I also learned about the skills of effective leadership such as chairmanship. I watched fabulous chairs skilfully begin meetings and draw them to a close on time and revelled in the fact that I had to concentrate to keep up in the agenda. The sheer speed but also inclusiveness of the chair was inspirational and appealed to my impatience and my need to be moving at pace. I honed my skills in those meetings, later became chief executive, and this remains an area of leadership I am proud to be involved in.

The first project – establishing an out-of-hours cooperative

At this point I was young, enthusiastic, and I went straight into partnership through a process of selection decided by dinner and a handshake. In my seat in the surgery, I continued learning more each day about clinical presentations, behaviours, and communication across the boundaries of lives, families, suffering, and sickness in one of the most deprived areas in the country. It was from this seat I started to think beyond the person, the room, the practice, and into the system. We were visiting and on call in unsafe areas until 10 pm and sharing weekends with another practice, which started to make me think about cooperation and collaboration.

Many practices were in a similar position, and although patient demand was low, the impact on family time was high. I started to imagine creative solutions.

On talking to the practice with whom we shared weekends on-call I found my first follower. He was a senior person, a counter to my youth, and helped me find favour and an audience. In my lunch times I visited practices to generate momentum, gain possible recruits, and whilst doing this, thought about the practicalities. Those were long days. It was a steep learning curve, a period in which I learned the importance of listening to discouraging voices. This helped me understand barriers to change, some personal and some structural, and really address them both through dialogue and through design.

I felt the sacrifices that I had to make. My thoughts had to be kept under wraps in order for me to cope with working full-time and I found myself unwrapping them at lunch, in the evenings, and all too often overnight.

Many tears were shed as my closest partners at work struggled to understand what was driving me and the decisions I felt needed to be made. Maybe I did not articulate this well. However, the experience helped me develop personal resilience which has served me well in my leadership journey. By resilience I mean the ability to avoid challenges impairing your mental health and avoid becoming so thick-skinned or scarred that you become closed to advice or unwilling to change your personal behaviour. This has been key in my personal development and has kept me sane along with emotional intelligence which, in my view, is one of the most important abilities.

Eventually the time came and the 'out-of-hours cooperative' was formed, my first ever new company listed at Companies House. The accountant who helped me became my lifelong friend. The new cooperative transformed the working lives of so many colleagues, bringing sanity to their work/life balance, and this made the personal sacrifices worthwhile. We went from

36 early adopters to 110 GPs in 1 year. In real life, I had my first child, and the Queen visited the service. All quite bizarre. The experience taught me the value of becoming aware of issues and creating solutions for them, sometimes doing this on the spot whilst holding the attention of a room full of busy GPs. I learned that part of my brain could become detached and watch the room, particularly peoples' faces and body language, whilst the other part was presenting. When questions arose, I learned to have dialogue in order to understand the issue better whilst thinking about the answer. Developing this capacity to be talking and thinking at the same time has proved to be a great tool.

I learned to value those who came to support me, as beyond the comfort blanket of trust they can be all you have.

Learning about power

The journey into more influential leadership territory was being formed. I began to realise that leading by hard graft, through earning respect and influencing others, is a bumpier road than leading by financial incentive or positional power, but this road is one I have grown to love. I view smooth paths as likely to be in the wrong direction. A smooth path is a path where it is easy to progress with little challenge, and this is often a sign that you are not truly making a transformative change. My journey continued through directorship and into merger, and I discovered that my ideals of honesty, integrity, and hard graft were naïve on their own and I had lessons to learn about position, power, and their effect on individuals. My fresh-faced view was about to change and my thin skin to be thickened by the greed, position, and in some cases the misogyny of others around me. I became better prepared through experience, but I also think that listening to the journey of others or having a coach or mentor in place can assist.

The company merged to deliver to a wider region, and I soon realised I was not tactical and was somewhat immature in the ways of business. The new company parted ways with my accountant, and I felt more distanced from the day-to day delivery of the service. I also felt the impact of being a woman in a man's world for the first time when at the directors' table. I continued a while but suffered as my passion was killed, the people I brought with me sought to further themselves, my friendships and relationships disintegrated, and I felt myself alone.

The environment felt toxic, and for my own sanity I left, keeping many secrets tightly to my chest and bearing the scars of them. I learned that position and pay can lead you to a place where you have to choose your path, which is that to move forward you either compromise your values or your income. The crossroads of truth and integrity with power or wealth. I chose to stay true to my values and left those who opted to prioritise income. I have quietly observed many others reaching the same crossroads in their walk and seen many make their choices. For me, I found freedom in walking away from compromise. I often encounter similar situations when mentoring, supporting, and observing others, and I believe that is when you know your shoe leather has been worn. I recognise what they are going through and understand, and it gives me the ability to support them using the treasure of experience.

After I left the cooperative, the thought of full-time clinical practice was too scary. I had recognised in myself that boredom was an enemy to giving my best and that I needed a pursuit which for me was a vision and goal for the system beyond my consultation room. I became a course organiser for training GP registrars with a desire and plan to tell GP registrars the things no one had told me. We met a day every week and we covered GP partnerships, contracts, business, and time management, not just consultation skills, disease, and its effects. They were challenging days as I had no academic background and little time to plan, but those heady days of discussion, provocation (mine and theirs), and developing shared belief systems were some of my happiest. I tested my theories of change management, I challenged and was challenged and still remain deeply proud of some of the leaders who arose from those groups, and I do allow myself to think I might have played a small part. Here was where quick thinking and presenting with empathy were practised and I came to rely on these skills later with huge audiences and on big platforms. Each week I further developed my ability to inquire, take challenge, and remain unoffended and unemotional. All people come from different places and different viewpoints and understanding people's views is the first stage in influencing them.

I pause here to consider how to identify things that sustain you. Be aware of and thankful for all the gifts you are sent along the way: a small letter of thanks, watching someone else flourish, a moment of clarity of vision, a companion on the journey for a brief time.

For 15 years I continued in full-time practice with evenings at the LMC and became vice chair, chair, and then as I thought my time was concluding and I was ready to depart from the LMC, leaving it in safe hands, I was drawn back due to circumstances and have remained as chief executive since. I have seen the rise of many, and sadly the fall of some, and have been privileged to play a part in the journeys of others.

System-level leadership – connecting with my drive

Devolution came to Greater Manchester in 2014 and, after I looked up the definition, I realised general practice and wider primary care hadn't been directly invited to take part. Based on a desire for the sector to be recognised and valued, I put on my tin hat and raised my head. The first battle for parity ensued with arguments made, swords drawn, and weapons loaded. It became a pivotal moment for the birth of the primary care provider voice and movement. At the time I thought all views would be calmly sought and supported, but later I realised how difficult this had been. We pressed forward and gained ground, and at times our troops were attacked from within as well as without. At moments we were few and surrounded, and other times armies appeared over the horizon to support us. We laid down weapons and instead used strategy. We aligned and grew in number. We formed and reformed. We hurt but we persevered. My understanding of the first follower, the lessons I had learned, the paths I had trodden before, now became alive, more alive than company and more real than words. The next 6 years are perhaps even a book themselves about relationships, values, and inclusion but deeply connected by vision, tactics, and sheer hard work.

I made the leap into senior management and at the time of writing, work for the majority of my week at the health and social care partnership as lead for primary care. I had to check my survival kit and learn to swim in a larger pool with hazards left and right but also sometimes with friendly currents. The survival kit was the tools I had sharpened in the earlier experiences: communication with empathy, calmness and interrogation of any challenge, close follower support, and a sack full of personal resilience. It was intense in terms of personal development, and the sheer amount of work to be done was colossal. It was great to feel part of a team again with a different skill set and focus, but it soon became a lonelier trail. This job brought me to a place where I called on all prior experiences and skills. These included creativity and vision to solve the problem of a disunited voice, strategy and tactics to ensure a voting representation, and some degree of parity for primary care. Added to these were the energy and passion to deliver a transformed way of working that could be truly provider led in a system that did not respect passion or representation. What struck me for the first 3 years was the change in the way that people approached me. Their behaviour showed me how many heads are turned by position and an office with your name on it rather than personal capability. I don't have an issue with position; my concern is more about how we socially interact with position. All leadership should be influential, but not all leadership needs to be positional. How we develop leaders depends on developing respect for others based on capability and not on a role that they hold. On leaving the senior management team after 3 years when funding was reduced, I noticed the same individuals immediately change their approach towards me, particularly in small behaviours which are much more revealing than the bigger statements. My note to self was to never be seduced by position and not to lose vision or purpose to maintain it, and also to endeavour to treat all individuals the same.

Through this time I observed a different territory: boardroom power play. It was a fascinating space for emotional intelligence geeks like me, and I found it fertile ground for experimentation. The scene begins with the hierarchy of who one greets or who greets you; it then matters where you sit or who cares to sit near you. It then speaks volumes who engages with you and who responds to you speaking to them. The boardroom tactical play often builds on hierarchy and intimidation and limits the inclusive contribution of many around its edges. A tactical rise for water or to take a call, the presentation of a paper to avoid exposure of detail, a change of order of agenda items are some of the tactics that may change outcomes in board meetings as much as the huddles outside the board. I observed unspoken dress codes for men and women, and those creating them and those following them. I recognised that pervading culture is in the small things. Understanding tactics is the first step in managing it as you see it and can then you can play a counter tactic or play to the same tune. Either way you are not surprised by the tactic, so its impact is lessened.

After 3 years I left SMT due to funding changes and my role was reduced overnight. There was no discussion, no debate, and no thought of the impact on me, as I went from 4 days to 2 in the same job. I decided to remain, as I had started, a more distant associate with the freedom to stay true to my values and represent my sector. I wanted to build a team with the right leadership aims and attitudes and to keep the vision of inclusive leadership by influence alive through open communication and respectful interactions. To build this team I needed more resources. Several attempts over long periods were knocked back, ignored, or changed until we agreed on a resourcing model. The use of a wider circle of committed individuals, working with national bodies and through our neighbourhood work it allowed for the national Primary Care Network contract to emerge.

However, things are never straightforward, and demolishing hierarchies is a tough sport. Long-standing influential leadership is a complex arena, and to stay trusted and connected is an ongoing challenge. The only tip I have is to always act in accordance with your values and with integrity. Do not compromise yourself, and always look to be encouraging others around you. People come alongside to be mentored or sometimes to usurp, and the only constant is continual change. The usurpers are often easy to spot, as if you are speaking with truth then they must oppose truth; if you are displaying good values then they are likely not. When challenge arrives, I try to be transparent and to use the experience to improve, but you can only be the best that you can be and control the things for which you have control. The greatest risk is not from those within but from those without who challenge inclusion and take opportunities to silence it or sideline it. So, by the time you read this I may be gone, but I hope my passionate value-driven leadership ambition will live on.

Commentary

Tracey seems to have learned her leadership skills the hard way. Like many who step towards leadership, she was initially driven by noticing injustice and wanting to play her part in addressing this. A burning sense of needing to address unfairness can generate a transforming energy inside us that is greater than any project or goal, no matter how laudable. As leaders it can be so useful to understand what energises us, especially when we feel we are running out of steam. As we mature, we often develop effective ways of managing our emotions, especially in how we handle issues that used to make us angry. Though this is a positive development in so many ways, it is helpful to keep in touch with our drive and the source of our energy.

Think about the last issue you really felt fired up about and how you harnessed the energy generated to help you to create a positive change.

Tracey describes some painful experiences, which had an impact on her, particularly at the start of her career but highlights the strength that can be gained when we are supported by someone who truly believes in us. Believing in someone is a powerful intervention that has been shown to have an impact on their future performance. Having someone who believes in us not only provides emotional support in the face of adversity but it also impacts on our self-view, helping us to recognise our strengths and unlock our potential for further growth and skill development. Sometimes we find this person in our work environment, and sometimes outside of it; both can be equally empowering.

Leaders who believe in their teams' abilities are generally more effective delegators and will reap the rewards themselves as their team flourishes. One common pitfall, however, is the impact of our unconscious affinity bias when we decide how we invest our energy.

We may find we are more likely to do this for individuals in whom we see elements of ourselves, and this can contribute to a lack of diversity in the leaders of tomorrow.

Think about the impact you may have made to an individual you have 'believed in'. What did you notice about their performance and development once they felt your support. Can you think of anyone you currently lead who might benefit from a greater sense that you 'have their back'? Particularly someone that you might have overlooked, maybe because of the affinity bias that we all have?

Although Tracey admits her dislike of prolonged reflection, she describes times when reflecting on her experiences had a significant impact on her leadership style and skills. Observing and reflecting on those leaders she admired helped her to recognise her impatience and her desire to lead projects at pace, thereby learning the skills needed for this whilst still aiming to include others in the process. This shows an awareness of her own needs (to act quickly). Understanding our needs as leaders can help us recognise there can be a shadow side to every leadership style. Pace can at times be the enemy of collaboration, as others need more time to process their thoughts and generate their contribution. This can create difficulties when team members don't know each other well enough to be able to adapt to the diverse personalities and communication preferences there may be in the room. This can result in dysfunctional meetings when either no one participates, or everyone speaks extensively but the discussion moves no closer to a consensus.

Are you aware of your leadership needs? Is it more important to you to get things done, or to bring everyone along with you? Whilst these things aren't mutually exclusive, the latter often takes more time and can be frustrating for those who like to move at pace.

Tracey recognises she gets her energy from a desire to make change outside of the practice and the consultation room. Doctors are often assumed to be driven by individual patient need although having a 'system view' may result in making a greater difference for a larger number of people. Certainly, leaders skilled in thinking of the wider system will play an important part in getting things right for the delivery of healthcare for our communities and to ensure resources are distributed fairly and spent wisely. At the same time, the health service needs leaders whose drive may seem less ambitious: to get things right on a smaller scale, both for the population they serve and for their team members.

Think about you own personal drive and ambitions. What level of leadership do you feel fits best with your needs and skills? How might this change as your career progresses?

Some of Tracey's more bruising experiences though her leadership career led her to develop a special type of resilience and a way of working with power that means she can fight the corner of primary care and the speciality of general practice in forums where the needs of general practice are not always understood.

She describes, in warlike language, the experience of fighting against the odds within a culture very different from the community she represents. Even though the values of those who have power within the system are different and damaging, she has shown how she can be successful, and that virtue, integrity, and inclusion will win out over the opposites. Even if we don't become system leaders, we will all work with people from different social or institutional cultures where painful clashes may occur and can learn to be better prepared and more confident in the power of compassionate leadership.

Within primary care culture we are generally expected to feel and show compassion, are naturally treated with respect within a system that we believe we understand and is stacked in our favour.

We are also required to tell the truth and not be devious and we assume that others do the same. Tracey shows that none of these can be relied upon especially when we work in different (system) contexts where the values are different and the basis of trust uncertain.

She has responded by learning the hard way through suffering by working in an unfamiliar and less supportive context. She has protected herself by learning personal resilience, and by being more politically aware and becoming familiar with tactics/power play. Once we become aware that the subtle behaviours of others might be a deliberate attempt to manipulate a situation or outcome, we then need to decide about whether we use the same techniques to support our aims. Whilst this may be a necessary evil in some situations where cultures clash, it is important to be mindful this is a choice, and not let it become a habit. Habitual tactics and power games, in settings where this isn't needed, can interfere with collaboration and genuine dialogue that may generate a positive endpoint that none of the participants had envisaged in advance. Remember that real listening isn't just waiting for our turn to speak and influence, but also allowing ourselves to be influenced.

Next time you are in a meeting with others, experiment with 'parking' any opinions you have on a topic until others have had their say. If they think differently from you, ask more about where their thoughts come from. Allow yourself to be influenced before you decide if you need to share your opinion, or if, after listening, you now take a different view.

Tracey has learned to sustain herself by not compromising her values; those of fighting the corner for primary care and ensuring the primary care provider voice is heard at all levels. This strong value drives her to keep going in the face of opposition or distractions. Strong personal values help to keep our leadership on track, and we can sustain ourselves by establishing strong connections with others who share our values, through real or virtual networks. Getting the balance right between the empowering force of a network of like-minded people and the harmful nature of 'group-think' when we can become entrenched in a binary viewpoint, particularly on social media can be a real challenge. It can feel safe and secure to surround ourselves with like-minded people but may limit us in understanding others.

Think about your own sustaining networks, including the benefits they bring to your leadership and resilience. Between them, do they challenge you enough to keep you broad-minded and adaptable?

Leadership at scale, especially at a system level, can be a cold and insensitive place. Such environments shape people in their image. We can survive and even thrive in them, but with care we can avoid becoming brutalised. Understanding our human needs, sharing some knowledge of our vulnerabilities with those whose support we would value, can do more than keep us going; it can keep us well. We all owe ourselves that.

Further reading from *The Leadership Hike*

Chapter 10 on navigating communication complexities and understanding power.
Chapter 16 on developing resilience and adapting to adversity.
Chapter 25 on maintaining integrity and authenticity when working in a wider system.

Podcast with the author

In this podcast, Tracey Vell shares how she learned to become a leader by listening to colleagues share problems and feeling the need to help find solutions. She describes her leadership journey as learning on the job and balancing multiple priorities as GP and other roles. Tracey highlights:

- The importance of curiosity and flexibility.
- How leadership at a system level differs from practice-level leadership, including an understanding of politics and making choices about your leadership interventions.
- How leaders can influence the environment or culture of the organisations they lead.

CHAPTER

9

Rupa Joshi

Dr Rupa Joshi is a Berkshire GP and primary care network co-clinical director. She has a number of roles in primary care transformation, learning, and development. Rupa's interest in lifestyle medicine and patient empowerment has led to transformational changes, catalysed by the pandemic crisis. In particular, Rupa has championed virtual group consultations (VGC) which help patients, ease workload, and are part of the changes in practice that clinicians are adopting.

I have been a GP for many years, and over this time I have witnessed increasing demands and complexity in primary care. A pattern was emerging. Patients were presenting time and time again. We were not getting to the root of their problems, nor addressing their concerns and what really matters to them within the 10-minute consultation. I felt it was time to change the narrative, to use a personalised care approach and help patients to make a difference to their lives by empowering them to self-care. I embarked on a journey of self-improvement, passing the BSLM/IBLM diploma in lifestyle medicine, and the ILM-5 to learn new coaching techniques. I aimed to motivate patients to make changes in their own journey of life. This personalised care approach, in turn, reduces GP attendances, and reduces the demand on colleagues.

As well as patient care, I was also becoming increasingly concerned about the welfare of colleagues. Demand was becoming unsustainable. Bringing joy back into practice, saving one GP at a time from burnout became a strong motivator for me.

DOI: 10.1201/ 9781003270492-10

I attended a training session on Group Consultations in 2017 and was bowled over listening to a patient talking about her type 2 diabetes QOF review. She talked of how she had felt isolated and didn't feel that anyone around her understood what it felt like to be living with diabetes. I was able to sense her loneliness. She was tearful and said that the group session had changed her life. She no longer felt alone and had met people who truly understood her day-to-day challenges. I realised at that moment that this was my goal; I felt inspired to bring this concept to our patients at the surgery.

The group setting enables patients to share their own personal experiences and decision-making; it allows the formation of a community of support, helping each other through small steps. The patients are empowered to share their ideas of what works for them in the management of their own long-term conditions. Listening to this lady talking so passionately about her delivery of care moved me and I, in turn, felt compelled to share this inspirational moment with others in the team. This sense of patient empowerment mattered to me in a way that it had not mattered before. I realised that the NHS was not providing group clinics as an accessible service to all. I felt energised to move this forward. This insight was what I had been searching for in order to give my patients the support and attention that they so desperately needed.

Back at the surgery, it was essential to engage the rest of the team: motivating and mobilising, establishing a shared purpose, leadership by all, using improvement tools and system drivers. I used the NHS Change Model for health and social care as a framework to ensure that I had considered all aspects in planning for the improvement journey. 'Our shared purpose' is essentially the glue that binds the model for change together.

I passionately shared my insights with our team, hoping to align hearts and minds with the idea, and understand our shared values, using the patient's story for inspiration. There was a sense of enthusiasm in the room, but quickly this excitement turned into questions on time and capacity, and how this would affect workload. I had anticipated these questions and reassured the team that a large number of patients could be seen at the same time, and it was actually time efficient. I sensed some scepticism, despite my best efforts to reassure. We reflected on the experiences of the diabetic patient. This was different to anything that anyone at the surgery had been involved in before.

There was an overwhelming sense in the room that there needed to be a change in how we care for our patients and that a 10-minute appointment was not enough time. We also discussed the benefits for clinicians. I knew that working as a team would improve morale, and we would be inspired by learning from each other and from our patients. The prospect of working together was something that the team were showing enthusiasm for. I asked all members of staff for their expressions of interest in being part of the group consultation team and nine members of staff, both clinical and non-clinical, put themselves forward. I was delighted! Our team then met regularly to set a strategy, and I used quality improvement tools at each step to guide us.

Inspiring a team to discuss their beliefs and values towards an improvement project when hearts and minds come together can be a magical experience, as I witnessed. This does take time to establish, which can be scarce in primary care. Asking a team what are the pinch points often works well as well as asking: What is the problem we are trying to solve? Will allocating some time help us to understand this problem more fully and therefore bring about a change to help us all? What is the hook for the individual team members? Will framing the problem be helpful? If team members are prepared to invest their time, their ideas, and points of view, they will be heard and they have the opportunity to effect change in a way that will help make their working day easier to manage. I found this to be the right path to follow to overcoming any resistance, and I could sense that the team wanted the project to succeed. It was a hugely positive experience working in a small team who share your values.

Paediatric asthma was chosen as our first group consultation. The team felt it was a good first start, there were easy to measure parameters, and it felt like a quick win to demonstrate to the rest of the practice team. High-risk children were invited. We made it a delightful experience for our whole team and the families who participated. We brought toys, games, and colouring for the children. Our group consultation team consisted of our finance officer as facilitator, our pharmacist, nurse, and me. The children were all aged between 4 and 6 years old. They were weighed and measured as they came through into the meeting room. The pharmacist then checked inhaler techniques and explained peak flow for the future. Nasal flu vaccines were administered. Each family was given an asthma care plan to fill out themselves with guidance and all questions were answered, forming a good discussion on when to call the GP, attend the emergency department and how to self-manage using their asthma care plan. The families formed their own WhatsApp group over the tea break. We continued with older age groups, each time becoming more accomplished with the process. I felt exceptionally proud of how far we had come in such a short time, and harnessed the energy from the team.

Our results were exceptional. We had small numbers, comparing one winter's results to the next. The GP attendances fell from 9 to 0, the emergency department admissions fell from 12 to 0 and the number of salbutamol inhalers requested fell from 18 to 8 following just one group session. The patient feedback and results motivated the team to keep targeting new groups as they saw for themselves the great impact we were making.

We continued with a cohort of six sessions in chronic pain management where we gained valuable insights into the lives of our patients and how they are affected. The patients chose the topics and we collaborated with our pain clinic consultant to attend one of the sessions. The information conveyed was much greater and richer than could have been achieved in a traditional consultation. I was overwhelmed with how difficult it was for this patient group to perform daily activities that I often took for granted. It was the first time I had truly understood their struggles. This experience changed the way I now consult with all patients with long-term conditions. Our mental health practitioner led a session on self-compassion and the concept of a hidden illness. Many of our patients found it difficult to make themselves understood to family, friends, and employers. There were good days and bad days when fatigue and pain took over and all they could do was rest. This often caused problems in their personal lives.

The patient voice was key to our learning as a team. We each played to our own and the teams' strengths. I learnt that leadership is about relationships and creating time and space to listen and be heard, being compassionate and thoughtful regarding each other's feelings, choosing your team, creating energy, understanding each other's motivations and how to influence the whole practice team.

One of my learning points was regarding pace-setting. I sensed there was a problem as the energy was low in our meeting, but nobody raised any issues when asked. After the meeting, I decided to speak to team members individually. I was very used to spinning multiple plates, working hard and at a fast pace. My father had always told me that you have to work twice as hard as a female non-white British person to be noticed, and this has always stuck with me. I realised then that not everyone is ready to go as fast as I go. This was an important insight for me. I realised that I would lose the team if I didn't change the time frames and workload. I needed to think about my own ambitions, perhaps I no longer needed to prove myself by working twice as hard. I needed to give myself permission to be the real 'me'. I decided to put the brakes on and make time for a well-deserved break over the summer holidays and start back fresh in the September. I could see shoulders drop when I approached the team; they needed a rest. This experience has taught me to be more in tune with the team and look for cues before stress and workload escalate in the future.

The staff also had other roles within the surgery team and resources needed to be balanced, particularly when staff were away over summer. I had to nurture my team and create opportunities for honest conversations and use coaching techniques to develop the potential of each member to form a stronger, more robust team. We were fortunate with the arrival of the additional roles reimbursement scheme into which we recruited a personalised care team to create a more targeted resource to specifically manage our group clinics. This started as a social prescribing link worker and health and well-being coach and has now expanded with the addition of a care coordinator and mental health practitioner. In addition, we also now have a Mind health and well-being worker, personal trainer, and project manager from the local council.

As part of my leadership, I have been curious about my own biases. As a doctor I noticed the assumptions about hierarchy in that the doctor is seen as the leader, having the final accountability. Working in this team challenged my own biases. I saw how patients were reassured, put at ease. The skills and manner that our voluntary sector workers, mental health practitioners, facilitators, and coaches had to offer challenged my assumptions. I felt that we all had so much to offer and everyone in the team was just as important and valued.

When Covid hit us, I wanted to reassure our patients that we were here for them and explain that we needed to adapt to new ways of working to keep both staff and patients safe. There were innovations in healthcare during the pandemic which would have taken years to embed, had we not had the freedom to adapt. As a result of these changes, there is greater accessibility and inclusivity. Some patients are now able to engage, where perhaps it wasn't possible before (e.g., online). There was also a need to change our topic focus, and we introduced new groups such as 'Covid-19 – A Medical Insight', Covid vaccinations, shielding, and a greater focus on mental health. During these times of high stress and crisis, I prioritised different leadership approaches, being more authoritative, pace-setting due to the rapidly changing environment. It was a chance to see the opportunities through the challenges, to communicate with transparency and to collaborate.

The team had gained momentum and energy. They were enjoying the sessions, learning and improving, and had many successes to reflect upon. We made a point of ensuring successes were acknowledged and celebrated in the team and beyond. We could see how the patients were connecting with each other and forming networks of support. I describe it as the 'light bulb' moment you have when you are having a meaningful interaction with a patient. Two minds connect; the patient feels as if 'You get me' and you are both on the same wavelength. This is very much what happens in a group consultation, but instead of just two people having this light bulb moment, you can see light bulbs going off all over the place, between clinicians and patients, and also between patients themselves. Once you have experienced this magic, there is no going back! This is what the team witnessed and had a sense of fulfilment, which kept their energy and motivation going.

Our feedback was excellent, and it was heart-warming to read some of the kind comments. I felt the team should celebrate their successes by having regular feedback reviews. We went on to do many more VGCs (virtual group consultations) and webinars and engaged over 700 patients from over 40 separate sessions. It has been useful to have documented all our improvement cycles. I have also been able to teach and advise others through webinars, observation, and quality improvement sessions through the Time for Care initiative.

At the surgery, we have twice-daily huddles where all staff discuss the current situation and challenges. I have used this to decide what the pressing issues are. Receptionist feedback has also been extremely useful. Democratic input empowers the team to tell us what is current and what patients are struggling with. I have found being honest and open about my own challenges has prompted others to open up and talk through their own challenges. It is also useful to have a flexible mindset and be open to ideas. If these ideas do not come to fruition, it is OK to learn from the experience and move on to something else.

Our VGC team formed from our 'burning platform' where we had a strong shared purpose during the Covid pandemic. We had to adapt to survive, as did the whole of general practice. It was important to create harmony in the team and build emotional bonds, ensuring that we all got to know each other's strengths and how we react in conflict. Meeting each other socially as well as at work was also helpful for building trust and really understanding our values and why we wanted to be part of this important work. During a crisis situation, these bonds can form quickly as we come to rely on team members within a short space of time and there is urgency in the response. Stress can also be a trigger for some, so it is also essential to create a sense of harmony within the team, encouraging people to talk about any concerns at an early stage and mobilising towards a vision.

It was a difficult time for NHS staff during the pandemic, particularly prior to the vaccine rollout. Not only were we dealing with sick patients, but also our own vulnerabilities. Many of our staff were shielding and working from home. There was a real fear of losing people close to us, our patients, but also our own families and friends. People were dying, a whole workforce was in unbearable pain, whilst still trying to maintain the care and attention required from the NHS, which we were all immensely proud to be a part of. I felt I had to maintain a safe, compassionate space for the team to talk about their feelings and deal with uncertainties. People needed support to manage the emotional burden of suffering and distress. This project was my way of coping with all that was going on around me and use stress as a driver. This was my contribution to the NHS in helping and caring for patients in a way where they still knew that we cared and were there for them.

There were many patient requests for appointments for orthopaedic pain (e.g., hip and knee), some of whom were on waiting lists for surgery. We had repeated requests for analgesia and to ask for expedition of hospital appointments. I contacted our local pain clinic consultant again, and we ran a session for our patients to self-manage their conditions. There are further examples of using VGCs as a platform for collaborating with other healthcare professionals, communities (Ramadan webinar), local council (long Covid, postnatals), and voluntary sector organisations (Caring for Carers).

We have organised VGCs and webinars for many conditions, including menopause, hypertension, and minor illness for under 5s. The mental health needs of our patients were escalating. The whole country was in a state of stress, so it was important to include sessions on anxiety, depression, and stress.

Changing the whole culture of a practice and primary care network has taken a lot of time and effort. It has helped that we have been successful in securing two separate funding streams and also utilised our 'additional roles' staff as an additional resource. Some team members are still not fully in support, and it has been a difficult journey getting others to see the benefits. Having multiple case studies published, featuring in the GP press, being shortlisted for awards, and having external validation from peers has helped bring credibility and influence. I no longer worry as I feel the impact now speaks for itself.

The team are now helping neighbouring networks to adopt VGCs. We have been funded to deliver postnatal VGCs and long Covid. The spread has taken much time, with many people at first saying that our resources were not being targeted effectively, and that VGCs were too time-consuming and not cost-effective. I sought comfort in learning about Rogers' diffusion of innovation curve. I had spent a lot of my effort and energy trying to convince 'laggards' of the benefits where my efforts should have been directed to spreading my knowledge to innovators and early adopters. If you have a new project which you think will work, don't be disheartened by those who do not believe in it. Find your tribe, enthuse those individuals who are willing to look at the project with an open mind, and show your passion and inspire others to succeed.

Throughout this whole process, I have become more confident, I've learnt from others, spent more time listening than talking, and increased my network. I tend not to get as stressed and take things more in my stride, remembering the bigger picture. I am a better timekeeper, open and honest, and have a much better understanding of my values. I have learnt that it is important to give people your full attention, have respect for those you work with, be prepared to change direction, and always follow through on your actions.

It has certainly been a journey. With any innovation, there will always be resistance to change. I met with resistance on time pressures and am still finding this now even after a few years of implementation. It is difficult to change mindsets and to ask people to step outside their mental valleys and think differently. Once the team is onside and sharing a purpose, magnificent ideas can flow with great enthusiasm.

So, my key insights are these:

- Leadership is about being true to yourself, working with people and delivering on a task. Be passionate about what you believe and find your tribe. Don't spend your time trying to convince 'laggards'.
- Utilise the skills in your team; everyone has their own skills, insights, strengths, and ideas. They all will have different styles of learning, so be sensitive and do not try and go too fast; be democratic. Our staff have enormous potential; we are all learning together.
- Make time for your team. Coaching individual members of your team will help them achieve their potential. Establish a shared purpose; be flexible and adapt.
- Communicate and listen with fascination to your team and your patients; be curious. Ensure that your change becomes embedded with regular email updates to the staff, having that change on the agenda of all team meetings. We also have a group consultation notice board to advise of upcoming sessions and dates.
- Have a project plan in place, using your QI tools, make it easier to do the right thing and harder to do the wrong thing.
- At the end of each session, ask yourselves 'What went well?' and 'Would it be even better if. . . ?' and use your insights to improve the next step.
- Utilise your support network and training resources. Join a relevant social media group and ask for advice. Prepare, read up, and anticipate questions.
- Don't be disheartened if there is a low attendance at your VGCs to start with; use patient champions, social media, local resources, and your entire team to spread the knowledge.
- Believe in yourself – you've got this!

Commentary

Are we making music together or just noise? In Rupa's open and heartfelt account, she relates the passion she feels for doing the right thing and the struggle that follows with getting others on board to play a new piece together. Let's take this aspect of teamworking further and think about motivation and the art of connecting with people well.

As leaders, we are often mindful of whether or not we are doing the right thing. Beyond the mechanics of doing what the job requires, we think about the bigger picture and whether what's important to the community is being adequately addressed. Leaders are not just moved by a sense of how what is already good can be made better. Even more so, they feel the emotions of shame, injustice, and so forth that come from recognising that 'things shouldn't be this way' and then use these feelings to give direction to the group and catalyse change. At least that's the theory, but how is it then that people don't simply agree with what seems self-evident and follow in the way we hope for or expect?

It helps to think about our mindset. Although it's natural to do so, we might succumb to our own myth of hierarchy, particularly as 'doctor leaders', and assume that we have the right, responsibility, and skills to lead. This is something that Rupa is careful to avoid. Not only may it be unwarranted, but it places us in a position of isolation with too much self-expectation of our limited abilities and not enough expectation of others. It can make us assume that the feelings that drive us will, or should, drive others in a similar way, which can then make us focus on projecting our own passion rather than hearing the thoughts of others.

We don't usually have a problem with those who feel as we do, but it can be tempting to characterise those who need persuasion as being difficult and thereby marginalise them. In fact, they may be doing us a service by pointing out the difficulties with the proposal or by suggesting other legitimate priorities. For example, they may argue that what is being proposed may not be part of the core business that we are funded for, which means the resources used on the new project could have adverse consequences for other parts of the service.

How do you feel about the doubters and naysayers? Even these words have a negative association, so what do you call such people in your own mind? How open are you to shifting your attitude towards them, and in what way could you think about them more constructively?

If such people are not moved by what drives us, it may not mean that they are ostriches burying their heads in the sand, but that they are thinking about other priorities. It can be helpful because it makes us more inclusive to remember that, when people don't agree, they don't have the wrong motivations, but maybe just different ones.

A different, less hierarchical mindset encourages us to step down from a conductor's podium and instead, think of ourselves being on the dance floor with our colleagues as a leader of the band. Change will happen anyway, but change that is musical rather than just noisy happens when leaders see the workforce, including themselves, as musicians who with judicious prompting and encouragement can play well together. As band leaders, we optimise change (i.e., make it 'musical') when we connect people in two ways: by connecting them to the music we're making together and also by connecting them to us, so that they feel comfortable to be directed.

Let's consider how we make these two types of connection in the world of primary care. Connecting players to the music means hooking them up to their intrinsic motivation such as those things they care about and are driven by. These might include what they value about work, what they are personally appreciated for, what they are pleased by or unhappy with, the types of problems or communities that they are concerned about, and so on.

There isn't a quick way of becoming aware of this, but the better we observe, the closer we listen, the quicker we get a feel for what drives individuals.

Who in your team do you have this feel for, a sense of knowing what they are motivated by and what makes them tick? Who do you not know in this way, and might that be a problem or a missed opportunity? Why? Who would you put at the top of your list to find out more about?

Beyond their values and attitudes, people are intrinsically motivated to do what they are talented in, so we need to become aware of (and use) their noteworthy skills, which may be beyond the skills they use in their current roles.

As we get to know more about individuals, we become much more able to tailor opportunities to what they might be motivated by and skilled in. In addition, the team can generate ideas about different ways in which a proposed change might bring opportunities for the practice beyond improving patient care. These might include financial opportunities for the business, better processes, increased efficiency and cost saving, changes that will help workload, well-being, and so on. Rupa gives a lovely example of this, whereby individuals who weren't necessarily hooked by the clinical benefits of group consultations were motivated by how these consultations could result in time being used more efficiently and workload thereby reduced.

We are supposed to be principally motivated by patient care, but what most motivates you? How do you feel about colleagues who are more driven by the day job and what they are measured on than any bigger picture or vision for the practice? How do you handle people who are a 'downer' on others, bringing people's spirits down through negativity or 'realism'?

Even before a problem has become crystallised into a proposal, leaders have an important role in making people aware of what may be coming. In this way, later discussions around what needs to change and who does what are not met with surprise or denial, both of which make it harder to feel motivated or take action. Of course, doing this in a way that raises awareness without unduly increasing anxiety is an art in itself.

Connecting people to their motivation is part of how we energise the team, and another useful way, as Rupa describes using the example of the pandemic, is how leaders opportunistically use sources of energy, like crises, to provide impetus and direction for the team.

Large-scale events like the pandemic are mercifully rare, but smaller crises that require urgent and concerted action are more common. How do you make use of these? For example, how do you get people to feel energised rather than drained of enthusiasm? How do you help them to feel confident to find a way forward?

We said above that the second connection that the team need to make in order to play well together is the connection to ourselves as leaders. Have you noticed how effective leaders very rarely use their nominal power to do this? People connect much more deeply and effectively if they wish to do so rather than because it is required of them. One of the most powerful feelings of connection comes when people feel appreciated or feel that they've been helped. Although we can show our appreciation in ways such as giving thanks and general praise, the types of appreciation that have more impact are the ones that are evidence-based. These show that we have noticed more deeply what they have done, perhaps recognising the challenges they faced and how what they did helped patients, colleagues, or both. Also, when we are in a position to help colleagues, doing so is a great way of creating the bonds that matter. Sometimes, appreciation needs to be given publicly. However, generally speaking, the more discreetly that appreciation and help are offered, the more likely people are to recognise that we are thinking of them and not about how we might look in the eyes of others.

These quiet acts of appreciation also help us grow as leaders, because they nurture our sense of humility as we learn to appreciate the value of others especially in relation to ourselves. We are touching here upon the notion of rank, which is pervasive because as humans we have a natural and immediate tendency to rank ourselves in relation to others in our community. This sense of relative importance makes it harder to connect with people we regard as being significantly less or more important. Being appreciative of others, like being kind to others, can be an antidote to this because these emotions connect people in a way that rank is not a significant barrier to.

The more we appreciate people for what they contribute and use this insight to include them, the more we recognise ourselves as one interdependent community. Where are you on this progression? You will recognise various tribes in the workplace, but how committed are you to showing them that beyond their differences, they need each other?

Once people feel connected to their intrinsic motivation and feel noticed and cared about by their colleagues, work feels less of an effort, and this can really help to sustain us.

The team is bigger than we imagine. Rupa shows us that patients who can help themselves are potentially a major contributor to the healthcare community; in fact we could legitimately think of them as team members. If we take the trouble to connect better with patients as well as with colleagues, then we can act as one community, each with different contributions to make to healthcare.

Even with this larger team, the improvements to our lives that we seek will never be easy to bring about, but will it feel less like labouring and more like making music? Well, the baton is in our hands.

Further reading from *The Leadership Hike*

Chapter 7 on how we can use quality improvement techniques to see if our efforts pay off.

Chapter 12 on keeping people on track and managing difficult behaviour.

Chapter 22 on understanding the problem before we attempt to fix it.

Podcast with the author

In this podcast, Rupa Joshi talks about virtual group consultations and being a lifestyle medic. She discusses:

- How she came to realise the importance of patient empowerment.
- How to bring people on board with change, including the sceptics.
- Why 'being a GP' is the most important foundation to becoming an effective leader.
- The power of routine reflection in shaping the leaders we could become.

CHAPTER

10

Craig Nikolic

Craig Nikolic is chief operating officer of Together First CIC, a GP Federation in the Barking & Dagenham areas of Greater London. He is a professional general manager with a very wide background ranging from the military via commerce to the NHS. Craig is also an IEEE professional engineer and has a special interest in health technology.

Going the long way round

I'm not exactly a leadership hiker, more of a rambler, and that shapes my perspectives on leadership. I hope to share these perspectives with you and help you improve your own leadership by applying a different external context.

This chapter will explore the learning experiences that have shaped my strengths as a leader, as well as the lessons I've had to learn through the years. Be aware, though: how I see the NHS is coloured by my life. Your own lens may be markedly different, and you may not immediately resonate with my views.

Who am I?

I'm chief operating officer of a general practice Federation providing at-scale primary care services to one of the most deprived areas of England. But this isn't about where I am now; it's how I got here and what I learned.

 DOI: 10.1201/ 9781003270492-11

My working life has gone from army soldier to leading artificial intelligence projects, to mergers with City law firms, to the NHS.

I didn't know what I wanted to do as a young teenager. The options for someone from a mining village in Scotland are limited, but I knew I wanted some adventure, so I joined the British Army. I spent 6 years in the army before leaving with a service-contributing medical discharge. This was a bitter blow because the army had become my core until I was injured in service and forced to change.

I didn't know what to do after that, but I was given advice to take time to adapt to civilian life. So, I did a law degree, thinking that I couldn't go wrong with one of those whatever I did. I did discover that I didn't want to be a lawyer!

Instead, I got a lucky break into delivering tech projects by someone who understood my transferable skills. Two years later, I was leading worldwide anti-fraud projects driven by neural networks. I was pioneering artificial intelligence work with some of the brightest minds I've met in my life. A forced change of job then came with my employer going bankrupt worldwide.

Again, I was given a break by someone who could look beyond narrow experience, and I joined one of the best law firms in the City in 2001, delivering worldwide projects, mainly mergers and organisational change, but also some strategy work.

Six years going around the world with them was enough for me, and I ventured out on my own to do some consultancy projects. The best fun was on a merger project between five law firms. I did discover that I don't like selling things, including my services!

Then my wife got ill. I got to see the dark side of the NHS, that it was essentially just a jumble of loosely connected organisations, stuck together by goodwill and general practice. I saw the impact of cuts and national policy. And I wanted to help.

A friend helped me into the NHS. I joined in January 2014, initially working on a project involving closing and splitting one multi-county organisation into 14 other existing ones. This experience and the fractured nature of what I saw made me even more determined to stay and help fix what I could; first as a deputy director of a commissioning unit, and finally on to where I work now. I'm now home in the NHS and an unashamed zealot for improving patient care. I'm settled and going nowhere!

In my career, I've also become a chartered professional, an IEEE engineer with a few sub-specialities, I've done postgraduate project management and management training, and I still have my bronze 25 m swimming badge somewhere.

I hope you can see that it's OK if you can't see a pattern in life; life is like that, and sometimes people follow successful non-linear paths.

I know my transferable skills and how to apply them to whatever challenge is in front of me. I also know what I am not good at and what I don't like. I like structure, I like delivering new things, I like seeing results. I don't like sales or bidding; I don't like stagnation or closed environments. By knowing those things, I can better marshal my resources and be a better leader. Do you know your innate qualities on both sides?

For people starting their career, mid-way through, or even approaching the twilight years, I hope I've shown you that the only thing stopping you doing something different is you. It's never too late to change career, after all I'm on my third major career change: military, projects/change, and now executive level management. Add to that the environments of army, engineering technology, City law firm, and now the NHS.

Breakout: looking beyond the CV

Have you given a chance to anyone you think has potential but may not quite fit yet? By only looking at a narrow pool, you are encouraging groupthink.

On the other side, how do YOU present yourself in a way that makes people look beyond their own narrow thinking?

What does the role really need? Does it REALLY need to be someone with narrow experience? In my experience, the only roles that require narrow experience are those bounded by professional regulation. Challenge yourself on both recruitment and jobhunting to look wider.

What have I discovered about how to lead?

What I aim to do for the rest of this chapter is to show you the biggest lessons on leadership that have impacted my career, concentrating on areas that people who've largely followed one career path may have missed. I'll split them into three broad categories:

- Leading from the past
- Leading today
- Leading for the future

Each of these has their own challenges for you; each gives you different opportunities. Come with me and join the hike from the past to the future.

Leading from the past

Leading from the past is a tell-tale of a leader who really understands the foundations of the leadership trade: learning from the successes and failures of the past to make tomorrow better.

It's a core element of military training, and any project management professional who doesn't do this doesn't deserve the title. It's the cornerstone of continuous improvement that many get wrong by treating it as a management task rather than one that shapes leadership.

Even the most junior of leaders can leverage this given its relative easiness to get right. By even acknowledging that you can lead from the past, you are doing better than many in influential leadership positions. Here are a few key lessons from my past.

You can't manage what you don't measure

Although I describe this in the language of management, it's leadership at its most basic, not leading your people into the same errors repeatedly.

I'm not talking about micromanagement, or unneeded bureaucracy, I mean looking at the choices you have made and learning from them.

The NHS hates doing this properly. With a passion. There's a love of targets, but not actually doing anything with them but micromanagement. There's certainly no leadership involved.

Proof: Show me a 'lesson learnt' or benefits analysis report from a project:

- That went well.
- That was a disaster.

If you're in the minority of NHS employers who do this routinely, congratulate yourself for choosing that place to work.

More proof: The NHS is full of people promoted or praised for grand projects that are never actually delivered or have failed to make the impacts promised. I doubt you have lasted more than a year in the NHS without meeting some of them. Look up, have a think about your immediate environment's leaders; what have they delivered? Is that REALLY what you want to be proud of in your career? Be better.

Learning from your successes

You've just delivered something amazing, it worked perfectly, everything fell into place. Do you know why it worked out this way?

What's the difference between this and other things you've done that were failures?

Could you do it again?

A scenario: I was managing the closure of a German global datacentre, moving all the data to the UK, all while having as small an outage as possible. The corporate cost of an hour without that data was £250,000. It went flawlessly. I could have just taken all the praise, but I was pushed by my then boss to dig into why, especially on things that only worked because of good fortune rather than planning. If I had to run that project again now, I'd do so many things differently, better, even though the original was a major success.

That's the heart of continuous improvement as a leader: reinforcing things that work well, as well as learning from those that didn't.

Learning from your failures

This is a fundamental skill as a leader. How you do this depends on your personality and environment. Some places thrive on it; others are ones in which admitting you've gone wrong is a career killer. The NHS has an institutional paranoia about admitting 'that didn't work' unless it's about someone who has already left, creating a convenient scapegoat!

Proof: Has someone senior, and currently successful, in your NHS workplace said 'sorry, I got that wrong' on something materially important? Good luck finding evidence.

I am naturally suspicious of people who refuse to admit when they've gone wrong, or when something under their authority goes wrong. These people are more likely to throw you under the proverbial bus to save their career than fix something that went wrong.

A scenario: In my career, I've made some huge mistakes, including jumping into one employer with a big name but awful reputation and thinking 'I can make this work'. I hated it, working with a director who wanted to act tough by bullying the ex-soldier. I left after 6 months and happily told everyone I'd made a mistake joining.

By looking back at what I really enjoy doing, what I do well, what I really dislike doing, and where I struggle, I now have a decent understanding of my work strengths and weaknesses. I wouldn't make it out of a similar interview these days without saying 'sorry, this isn't right for either of us'.

Here's my rule for someone working with me who makes a mistake:

- Was the mistake made in good faith? Did it go wrong despite their best efforts? If made in good faith, then help them make it better for next time. Help them learn and encourage them to admit problems; you'll find it reduces errors because people aren't afraid to ask for help sooner rather than when it's too late.

- Was the mistake made in bad faith? Given their skills and experience, should they have OBJECTIVELY known it was going to go wrong but did nothing about it? If so, that's a different conversation, including looking at the wider environment to ensure they could have spoken up earlier. For example, does the prevailing culture stop people speaking up? Are they afraid to speak up? Is the problem you, not them? A good leader knows that it's not all sunshine and that leadership will involve protecting the rest of the people who follow you.

It's a lifetime of work; you get better at leading from the past by continuous improvement – an art rather than a science.

As a leader, if you show you're restless with the same standards, even good ones, you encourage others to do the same. If you show yourself as closed to improvement (e.g., 'We're already perfect'), then you encourage ambitious others to mirror you and hide their own errors.

There is a shadow side to the above paragraph. It can be tiring to work in an environment that never settles. This is where your leadership skill shows: you can make continuous improvement business as usual. It's tough to start, but these environments are often the best and attract the best people. That's leadership at its most fundamental.

Leading today

Short-term leadership of the decisions you make today is where a leader proves their agility, flexibility, and empathy. It is a different leadership mindset than learning from the past. Hands-on and fun, as every day is different.

This is where the NHS really goes wrong. It removes the authority of managers to lead. It gives them a narrow box and expects people to stay within it.

Leaders aren't allowed to lead

The NHS is terrified of making decisions, it forces things through committees, or to the highest level possible, and overwhelms those people with decisions outside their skillset.

Proof:

- Can your local Trust's chief executive sign off on free milk for staff tea or coffee? Most can't. Seriously. (Close your shocked mouth and keep reading, it gets better).

- Next time you get a decision turned down, look at the language used. Is it 'they' who won't allow it? Or a named individual? 'They' means the person conveying the decision doesn't want challenge.

The best companies in the world are the best because they actively encourage innovation and personal leadership; they delegate leadership powers down to the most junior staff.

Kodak, once a world-leading company and seemingly invincible, refused to innovate and shut it away at board level. They went bust, deservedly. I do not see the difference between Kodak failing and many parts of the NHS, the latter only surviving because they're 'can't fail' statutory bodies.

Let people lead (existing leaders)

Subtly different to the above, this is where YOU set people free. Lead by encouraging people to take responsibility. Narcissists do this but then steal all the credit for themselves. This is where you go a different way.

Here's what's in it for you. If you allow someone to lead and give them the credit for their successes, they'll keep doing more. Think how easy your job becomes if other people solve your biggest problems for you.

An example: I was managing a major merger; it was very tight in terms of the budget we had. My leads had autonomy and encouragement to do things better. One, a junior person in his first leadership role, took me at my word and came up with a completely revised plan for his part that saved £2.4 m by removing the 'we've always done it this way' fuss. He got all the credit, but I also looked good in my results.

A second: Remember that German datacentre project above? On go-live night, I was teaboy and pizza delivery man, and between that I watched a couple of movies at my desk. My people were more than good enough at leading their teams; they didn't need me hovering. They knew I was there if they needed me, but also that I trusted them to get on with decisions that could cost millions if it went wrong. If you act calm under pressure, it has a calming downstream effect on those who choose to follow.

I trusted them to lead.

Let people lead (everyone!)

What would your NHS organisation do if a janitor said, 'I know how to improve patient care'? Would they ever even be heard beyond their own supervisor who'd encourage them to stay in their lane? Would they be patronised into never speaking up again?

The NHS believes leadership authority equals clinical grade and managerial rank, and that's about the most stupid thing that any organisation can do.

Leadership can come from anyone. A junior person standing up and doing the right thing at significant personal cost. The CEO setting a personal example on an ethical and moral stance. A junior doctor putting in an anonymous whistle-blower report while staying to work in a toxic environment because the patients need them.

Very few places do this well, and the NHS is notorious for its rank and professional snobbishness.

Empower every single person by daring them to lead and improve.

Leading by listening

This is where you can lead at your most effective level.

You listen.

Pay attention to what people are telling you, whether they're a patient advocate being ignored, or people tweeting that they can't get a hot meal at 3 am while on shift.

If you're hearing nothing, then either you're not listening, or worse, your staff have given up on you listening.

This is especially important when it comes to equality and diversity. Does everyone look like you, or have a similar career profile to you? Are you listening to anyone different to you in life experience? Through their silence, they may be telling you that you're just not listening.

This is a legacy from my army career. The worst thing possible for a leader is a soldier who isn't complaining about something; it usually means they've something major that's upsetting them, but you've missed it.

Not only will listening properly help you with problems, but it'll also help you spot opportunities. Consider asking people, 'What do you think of . . .' when you have a new idea, then stop and properly listen. It's harder than you think, listening to non-specialists on a subject you know well, but it can often give you a completely new context.

I encourage my teams to ask 'Why?' on everything. It forces me to justify decisions and think through scenarios, especially if someone can't understand the 'why' for a decision. It makes for more rounded decisions. Many things that I've done that make me look good are because someone has helped me think it through properly.

Leading for the future

OK, you've looked back, you know what you're doing now, but the future is a fuzzy uncertainty. How do you lead for that? This is the hardest part to do properly.

Weak leaders hide behind uncertainty. Stronger, fairer leaders embrace it.

Managing uncertainty

The NHS struggles to manage beyond a year ahead; 3 years ahead is a long-term strategy. Even then, it would be pencilled in because you won't know finances until just before the new financial year.

Did you know that a successful large commercial company would consider 3 years as a short- to mid-term strategy?

How can you lead if you don't know where you're going?

Your first task is to know what plans exist and to understand them at a level that helps you lead others. You must know enough to understand the gaps, and what you can do about them.

There's no point charging into a dead-end, or something that won't exist tomorrow.

Then you show people a vision of a future embracing that uncertainty. Paint them a mental picture of an objectively reasonable outcome. Make it theirs to own.

Understand your own experience

By the time you get two to three decades into a career, you are innately using your applied experience and knowledge. At the start of your career, you have nothing but your personal attributes. That's fine. If you're aware of it, you can manage it. What works for you may scare others.

On the other side, everyone knows a 'Yes, but' leader who tends to be a doom-monger; don't let that be you. Use your experience to find a way through; and if you can't, let others lead if they can do it better.

Foundations for the future

In the NHS, you can get all the way to chief executive level without a single leadership or management course. If you're lucky, you're trained on the job by people with their own leadership style. Poor practice is baked in, and it's noticeable to those who come in from outside.

As a soldier in the British Army, you're not just expected to be able to lead at your current rank, you're expected to understand the job of the next rank up. You're trained hard, you cannot rise in rank without being expected to learn more about command, leadership, and management.

One of the first things I did when I joined our current board was to find money to train our largely clinician board in their role. We did the Institute of Directors Certificate and only Covid stopped us doing the Diploma that would have given them Chartered Director level training. For some, this was the first proper management training in their career.

'I'm not training them because they'll just leave' is the rallying call of scared leaders.

Beg and borrow money to train your people; be a vocal advocate of learning: you're investing in the NHS of tomorrow by leading today.

Putting it all together

Through my career, the best leaders I've seen are those who are impatient with the status quo of yesterday, who can paint a picture of the future, and have the leadership agility to do things about it today.

I've tried my best to live up to that and have learned that it's achievable by anyone willing to put the effort into building the experience to make it work. It's not a labour of a few days, it's a lifetime of opening myself to being better tomorrow.

Now, what are you going to do tomorrow?

Commentary

Vive la difference! You may have noticed that many times in this book, we refer to the importance of including and taking notice of people who are different from ourselves. We've said that they bring an alternative perspective which is uniquely valuable, and Craig is a shining example of this. We mean 'shining' literally, because people who come from a different background can shine a light on things that are so much part of our way of life that we scarcely notice them. With Craig and his spirit of adventure, we see through his eyes how we are unhelpfully restricted in our world, with many of those restrictions being self-imposed. Of course, Craig will have restrictions of his own, but the point is that he comes in to healthcare less constrained by our norms and expectations and is able to see how these affect us. That's an enormous help.

We often recruit people who have come from diverse life backgrounds, perhaps different organisations. Do you make use of this, especially when they are new to your community, to find out what they see with their 'fresh pair of eyes'? For example, do you ask them after a short period of bedding in, to feed back both on things they see going well that we could share with others and also on things that surprise them, or that they don't see the reason for?

Diversity of thinking, perspective, and strengths is vital to us. As Einstein said, 'You cannot solve a problem with the same mind that created it'. Hence, people's differences are not a threat but an asset, but as well as recruiting people from diverse backgrounds, we can make much better use of the diversity already present in our teams.

Liberating this diversity requires us to appreciate that people have far more bandwidth of ability and potential for growth than we ever make use of. This process of liberating others starts with liberating ourselves.

Craig's own life story shows the freedom and fun that come from having a different attitude to progress in life. We don't have to think predominantly in terms of career, roles, or rungs on a ladder. These are the surface contexts in which we apply ourselves. Instead, if we gave more significance to what lies beneath the surface, such as what we have learned about our personalities, strengths, and problem-solving, we can use these to guide us. For example, we can bring ourselves to the job rather than just the job to ourselves, thereby shaping the way we do things so as to make better use of our strengths in meeting the needs of the present. The alternative, which is to disregard our strengths and do things as they have traditionally been done, sounds like a wasted opportunity but is what many of us do by default.

When Craig talks about being comfortable with a non-linear progression in life, he is pointing out the freedom that comes from allowing ourselves to grow, to become a good fit by adapting and shaping ourselves to our opportunities, rather than hope that the future will fit us as we are. Craig points out that unless there are regulations that dictate otherwise, we have far more freedom to grow and to change our circumstances than we make use of.

How much is this part of your mindset? Do you recognise how you are growing, for example what you are learning about yourself and your skills? What impact does this have on the significant life decisions that are made about your future? As a colleague or employer, do you encourage others to think this way? What effect are these attitudes having on you and your organisation: are people flourishing by design rather than by chance?

We mentioned 'becoming a good fit'. This relates to us personally but also relates to helping each other to become good fits by raising awareness collectively. Craig mentions the importance of understanding the role of the rung above, but maybe other rungs need to be understood to a useful degree. Why? Because by understanding each other's circumstances, we can work more effectively and considerately together, avoiding some of the unnecessary distress that results from ignorance and misunderstanding. Sharing these insights doesn't come easily or naturally and leaders can help a lot by promoting both the language and the culture of feedback for growth.

People don't always recognise what they are doing and how this helps or hinders the team. Do you help people to (in particular) understand their strengths and how the organisation benefits from their attitudes and abilities? For example, do you point out to them 'I noticed you did. . . . It was really helpful because . . .'.

Do you think about how you can make better use of the strengths that you notice in people, maybe by creating new opportunities for them within existing roles?

Any opportunity for an individual to grow is an opportunity for the organisation to grow. If we can see that, it means that we need no longer fear, as some organisations do, that providing training and support will simply result in good people leaving.

Let's think further about fear. Fear constrains people, and this inhibits growth and the creativity and fun that goes with it. We've established how important listening is in helping people to feel connected through being heard and taken seriously. But what if people aren't being listened to because they aren't being allowed to speak? As Sheinaz Stansfield pointed out in her chapter, artificial harmony is toxic. Craig highlights this, too, and how hearing complaints is a sign of health, not disease.

Creating a safe environment and encouraging complaints and niggles doesn't just happen. It needs those with power to encourage and support it. If the culture is one where managers can't 'sign off on free milk' or where people see that cutlery or mugs are missing but never get replaced, then empowerment is missing. People are unhelpfully constrained and the responsibility for this lies with the leadership. Why? Because at its root, we want to create organisations where it's easy for everyone to do what is jointly recognised to be the right thing. Leaders shape that culture. This might mean, for example, having clear processes for replacing broken or missing items or having positive attitudes to those who are trying to make things better but maybe have gone about it the wrong way.

What is your attitude to the grumbles in your team? Do you take notice of these and do something about them or do people stop complaining because nothing happens?

Attitudes are fundamental, and as leaders we have subtle but powerful ways of making it clear what we are prepared and not prepared to hear. An example of such an attitude is whether we are seen as pessimistic or optimistic. The latter is perhaps more common because leaders are generally energised and looking to change things for the better. This might sound like a good thing, but it can have a downside because it can be very difficult to say negative things to optimistic people. As 'positive' leaders, we might shut others down, maybe not explicitly, but through our reputation and particularly through our body language which says 'Don't tell me about the bad stuff'.

Trying to balance who we are by trying to be the opposite generally doesn't work. For example, it's hard for an optimist to think pessimistically. Instead, a useful way forward is to use curiosity to find out more, which allows people to open up without worrying how we might take it.

How do you show curiosity? Keeping the enquiry neutral may mean saying 'That's interesting, tell me more' rather than 'That's really good'. Have you checked your body language so that you are not saying one thing and signalling another?

Changes in behaviour like this can really help leaders not to fear hearing things that we may previously, with a less neutral attitude, have found difficult, dangerous, or damaging.

Craig takes this a stage further in the wider issue of our attitude to the information that comes from data and in particular, measurement. What people have to say need not be feared. We can say the same about measurement, whilst not being naïve about it. Measurement is partly used for accountability and censure and in these situations, it would be foolish not to think carefully about how we collect and present the information. Income, viability, reputation, and position depend upon these, and it becomes natural to fear measuring anything that might show us in a poorer light.

However, there is a wealth of measurement that we can undertake for our own purposes and that doesn't have to be reported upwards. This helps us with the continual task of quality improvement and takes some of the guesswork out of making changes. Indeed, it is the information that 'shows us in a poorer light', that we often learn the most from. It would be damaging for us to fear doing this and to tar 'data collection for quality improvement' with the same brush as 'measurement for accountability'. If we aren't careful, we can forget that data is a piece of chalk from which we can learn, not just a stick that we might be beaten with.

Craig is illuminating and, like a torch, the light he shines from a different perspective chases our shadows away and makes us feel less fearful and more adventurous. And as Craig shows, freedom isn't just a nice idea, it's where joy lies – and what is life without that?

Further reading from *The Leadership Hike*

Chapter 2 on leadership in the modern world and how management and leadership are related.
Chapter 6 on not just fitting in to what's expected.
Chapter 16 on the art of being more adaptable.
Chapter 23 on measuring for improvement, not just accountability.

CHAPTER

11

Krishna Kasaraneni

Dr Krishna Kasaraneni is a GP in Sheffield and, after graduating from Leicester, came early in his career to a significant role in medical politics. He was a member of the British Medical Association's GPs Committee and then part of the GPC Executive Team, where he represented the profession especially in its negotiations with government. Krishna chaired the BMA's Equality and Diversity Committee and has particular interests in the development of GP workforce, health inequalities, and shaping a sustainable general practice.

Why am I sharing my experiences of a career in medical politics with you? What makes it worth sharing? I was fortunate enough to have played a role in representing the profession for just over a decade, and it has certainly been an interesting one. I was able to observe, learn, and experience what leadership looks like, especially in a time of adversity, and that is why medical politics is relevant even for someone like me who has very little interest in politics but has always been fascinated by leadership. My involvement included policy creation, implementation in medical training, pensions, equality and inclusion, premises and infrastructure, pay, research funding, and many other things at the British Medical Association.

The health service has been in crisis for as long as I can remember, and that has been the overarching theme of my time in medical politics. I spent about a decade in the thick of things, and what I have described in this chapter may come across as ramblings of a 'has-been', and they probably are to some extent. What I hope is that it allows readers to share some of my experiences and learn from them rather than to live them all themselves.

DOI: 10.1201/ 9781003270492-12

This piece is my reflection on a journey that involved more ups and downs than I ever imagined, and a feeling that it leaves me with: a huge imposter syndrome.

Principles

This may sound a little obvious, but the reality is that without a sound set of principles one will struggle in medical politics. The principles don't necessarily have to be ones that you start off with, but they need to evolve and continue to be refined very early on. Reflecting on my own journey, I wanted to do my bit to protect the NHS during the great turmoil over a decade ago when the health service was being completely deconstructed. Thinking about it now, this did result in positive changes in some aspects of the health service – like introducing clinical leadership at the heart of local decision-making. However, the changes also allowed a significant part of the NHS to be broken into parts and brought a new meaning to 'competition' in the health service. How would I approach changes in health service organisation second time around? I would be more balanced, rather than focusing only on the things that I saw as threats.

The other important issue that I struggle with every day is how to balance my personal views in a medical political world when the colleagues I represent have such diverse views, some of which are diametrically opposed to mine. I believe in a state-funded national health service that serves the people in the way Bevan described it. But it is not unreasonable to find that others don't share that view. Being open to a diversity of views is very important in any journey in leadership. Only when one can see and understand how others view a situation/problem from different perspectives can one truly lead. Dismissing opposing views and losing the support of colleagues who hold strong views (even in complete contradiction to your own) is probably the easiest way to fail as a leader.

It is also imperative that one recognises that having some who may not share your principles and who frequently disagree with you does not make one person right and another wrong. Finding common ground is a better way, one that takes on board what we learn from opposing positions. The more open you are about diversity of thought and recognise that people are allowed to have different views, the more you find yourself agreeing with 'others' and seeing things from their points of view. I doubt anyone will ever get the balance right, as it is not in the human psyche to agree with opposing views all the time, but if you are open to listening to what others have to say, you have a better chance of influencing them with your ideas.

Purpose

As with the principles, it is important to recognise what motivates you to get involved in medical politics. I've seen people who want to get involved as they have a personal ambition to get to a certain place in terms of title and recognition and I have also seen individuals who got involved because they have a purpose that involves helping others and helping the profession. It is important to recognise that altruism on its own cannot be a sole purpose. You must have an individual purpose along with the desire to lead. There is nothing wrong in wanting to improve things for others as well as making your own life a little better. This can translate easily into clinical work too. For example, I developed an electronic tool that makes the management of lipid abnormalities as easy as clicking a button. It improved patient care, and just as importantly, it significantly decreased the workload for clinicians in this area. In this scenario, it's difficult to say which 'purpose' was the right one – improving patient care or decreasing the workload for colleagues. Is it important to make that distinction? Probably not. If the purpose is clear, leading and implementing change becomes more straightforward (for us).

Having said that, once you get into the thick of things, it is quite easy for the process to take over and you might forget why you were there in the first place. Never-ending meetings and discussions can take over the task at hand, which could end up taking a back seat. I certainly noticed this in people who had been involved in national roles for a very long time. The only way to deal with it is to not see medical politics as a career but to give yourself a period of time after which you will walk away.

Involvement in medical politics is about influencing positive change for the colleagues you are representing, and not about changing yourself beyond recognition. So, listen to others, constantly correct your course, and be prepared to be right at some times and wrong at others, but always to have a strong purpose for what you want to achieve. Then, you will actually be able to hear your peers and make small positive changes even if the benefits aren't obvious or quick.

On a personal level, having a clear purpose relatively early on certainly made my experience a positive one, and one I look back on with fond memories as well as some bruising ones. As somebody who didn't really have a personal ambition in having a career in medical politics, I found it easier to get involved when I felt I needed to. And on reflection, I also found it perhaps a little easier to walk away from, because I didn't feel too trapped by the position or benefits. It also helped that I felt that my purpose was to do what I was able to do and that staying involved beyond that point would risk denying someone else an opportunity to get involved.

People

It's difficult to think how/when my journey in medical politics started precisely. I remember entering an election in my first year at medical school to represent my peers and that, I suppose, could have been the beginning. Why did I put myself forward, and what did I care about? I don't think I knew exactly what it was at the beginning, but it is becoming clearer, and the answer is simple and has always been in front of my eyes – it's people. It is about giving a voice to peers and making a difference. Once you realise that being in a leadership role is not just about all the wonderful things that you can do for people when you are in a position of power, you will learn to set your goals in a realistic way and start working through them systematically.

Leadership is also about learning from people who inspire you. For me, the inspiration was a Lancashire GP colleague. He spoke up for the founding principles of the NHS at every opportunity and I basically wanted to be like him when I 'grew up'. And as luck would have it, I ended up working very closely with him for most of my time at the BMA.

When it comes to working with people, medical politics makes it impossible to get things right for everyone. So, don't even try to. You will find that many people will have views that are directly contradictory to others and people seldom change their views over time. I do feel that this is something particular about medical politics, as it affords an opportunity for some to become 'champions' of a cause that others can get behind, but one they know will never be realised. For example, it is very easy to say, 'give us more money so that we can do our jobs better'. Who would disagree with that? But how easy is that to achieve?

In those situations, oddly, the people who evolve their thinking will be seen as the problem and not the ones with rigid views. Some of this will be down to the self-selected nature of people involved in medical politics, who are there because they have something to say. And inadvertently that means they may end up with less bandwidth to listen to others. The ones who succeed in my view are the ones who listen first and talk later – there is nothing wrong with course correction.

When it comes to decision-making processes, medical politics is not necessarily about acting in the interests of the majority of the people all the time. You will find yourself making decisions that are sometimes about protecting the most vulnerable or a very small minority because it is not necessarily about equality of opportunity every time. It may be about *equity* of opportunity and representation and that means sometimes having to look out for the 'little guys' and making sure that the decision-making processes don't inadvertently disadvantage the minority or the ones who are already struggling. For example, taking a very urban-centric view in policy-making may please the majority as most of the profession work in urban or suburban areas. But, what about the impact of that type of policy in rural and deprived parts of the country? Not all deprivation is inner-city focused; there is the issue of rural deprivation that does not get enough attention. It is important, therefore, to consider policies that are equitable and don't widen the inequalities that we live and work with, rather than accepting the majority view as gospel.

Popularity

Do not confuse leadership with a popularity contest. You can be popular by saying all the things people want to hear, but not actually delivering any of them and blaming it on someone else. But you will achieve nothing that way, and the colleagues you represent will not see the difference that you promised them in your election statement. If you don't have thick skin, you may want to reconsider a career in medical politics.

Whilst the attention received by getting involved in medical politics may appeal to some, it may mean making decisions that will be unpopular at certain times but are in the interests of the profession in the long term. That's why, for the principled few, the journey in medical politics always ends in 'defeat' if you consider it a career. I realise that it paints a rather sombre picture, but when it comes to medicine, and general practice in particular, the diversity of views across the profession means you will never be able to take everyone with you. Whatever decision/direction you try to lead the profession in, even with the most noble of intentions, there will be people who will not share that vision. That is the most important thing that you need to reconcile with if you venture into leadership roles in medical politics – you won't please them all, and you shouldn't try to. You could take the alternate approach of speaking up as a popular voice, but avoid getting involved in shaping policy, guarding yourself from the criticism, but I would argue that it defeats the purpose of getting involved in the first place.

Patience

Looking back at my journey so far, I think the biggest lessons I have learnt are to be patient and actually make mistakes. The medico-political world is full of people with strongly held views who believe their views to be right and who almost universally disagree with others who do not share their way of thinking. That is a huge challenge for leaders in the current climate. Trying to gain consensus and finding middle ground is almost impossible as someone will always disagree with the decision that you made. And over a relatively short time span, you will find that inevitably most will disagree with some of your decisions/views. You will find yourself in a position where you have to win through and prove a point through a variety of means – persuasion, and dare I say 'strong' persuasion in some instances. And one needs patience to make that happen. That is also the way to convince government and others who actually hold the 'real' power, which is a lot harder than simply making loud and powerful statements.

In reality, the outcomes of changes in policy and decision-making can take a significant amount of time to bear fruit, and this could be the downfall of some individuals who expect quick results in terms of changing government's or policy makers' thinking. The work that I did on workforce in general practice took at least 5 years from creating policy to convincing politicians to implement change and finally starting to make a difference on the ground. How do you measure the success of your work in such a short space of time? You don't. Whether you get it right or not depends on the 'majority' view when it comes to measuring success. And different people will use different markers to measure success, so do not be disheartened if others expect something different. This is something I took from clinical medicine into medical politics – a diagnosis is not obvious the first time someone presents; using time as a diagnostic tool is not that different to using time as a negotiating tool.

Priorities

As Frederick the Great said, 'He who defends everything, defends nothing'. Whilst a battle analogy is not the best comparator for medical leadership, it does sum up the challenge in representative politics. As I mentioned, colleagues will have different views and priorities, and what becomes more important when representing such a diverse profession as medicine is that the work is spread out and work is undertaken as a strong team, with individuals focusing and prioritising different areas. The cliché of there is no 'I' in the team is a very real concept in medical leadership. Do not try and do everything yourself – you simply won't be able to.

This is also an area where conflict arises. What is a priority for you will not be a priority for someone else. What is a priority today may not be a priority in a decade's time. Things evolve and you need to evolve with them. A good example would be to look at the store Blockbuster – can you really see them in the high street now continuing to rent out VHS tapes and DVDs as they did 30 years ago?

Therefore, you need to prioritise, evolve, delegate, and 'team up' to make a difference in the world of medical leadership.

Passion

This has been a constant throughout my career in medicine, and this is probably what will remain with me for as long as I am a GP. The persistent passion and having a vision for the future (where the reality of working in general practice is that it is not always about doom and gloom and putting fires out every day) is what motivated me to get involved in politics.

Passion doesn't mean we simply focus on pay and rations; it is about looking around us and making everything about a career in medicine a meaningful vision. Whether the vision is about bolstering the current model or supporting the new ways of working, passionate advocacy of the profession is about bringing everyone with us, helping them heal and bringing hope to them. Fundamental to passionate leadership is about making our voices heard with coherence and impassioned clarity and persuasiveness. We need to heal and come out of the current crisis with a future that we can all feel optimistic about – one which, with a hand on our heart, we can talk up to the trainees of the future.

That passion also needs a variety of complementary attributes to translate into meaningful change. A career in medical politics needs passion that is complemented by excellent communication and networking skills and the ability to command the respect of both colleagues and opponents. None of that is easy, but it is a must. It needs to be done in parallel by maintaining the respect of colleagues, policy makers, allies, ministers, MPs, civil servants, and managers. You can disagree with them, but you need to maintain civility and respect – a mutual one.

As I reflect on my role in representative politics it does make me wonder about the areas that I was able to progress and the areas where I wasn't able to. What certainly got me through some of the most challenging times was the team around me. And that team should not be about having like-minded individuals around so that your views can be reinforced. I've had the pleasure of working with experts in health policy, economics, public relations, lawyers, and accountants and many more who always knew more than me about most topics. It is therefore imperative that you don't walk into medical leadership thinking your views and your ideas are the best ones and that you have all the answers from the outset. My most productive pieces of work were done in conjunction with subject matter experts in those areas. We would argue and discuss things and reach consensus and come up with a well-rounded argument or a policy statement. I enjoyed it when people half my age were challenging me on my strongly held personal views and my way of thinking about what the priorities are. I enjoyed it less with those who took the default position of disagreeing just because they wanted to – I tried to stay away from them.

What would I say to my colleagues who are thinking about venturing into medical politics? Here are the five things that got me through:

1. Don't think of it as a career – think of it as an experience. If the objective is to get to the top, you've lost even before you've started.
2. Stick to your principles but be prepared to listen to alternate views and keep refining your thinking.
3. Be prepared for personal attacks – when people run out of policies to attack you on, they will turn personal. If you don't like confrontation, this is definitely not for you.
4. It can become all-encompassing, so make sure you draw your boundaries to keep the work-life balance in check.
5. Don't expect to be loved/popular in medical politics, particularly representative politics. This is not a very glamorous role, and it certainly isn't going to win you accolades – it's hard graft, so do it because you want to. And when that desire stops, you need to stop and move on and let someone else have a go. Don't end up a dinosaur.

If you are going down this route, try to be fair and remind yourself frequently of your values. Do not surround yourself with people who agree with you but be bold enough to be challenged. It can become a toxic environment, and the strong passion may draw you in even further. If you are going to make a go of this, you need to be able to live with it. I was able to for a period of time, but that period of time was finite.

I would end by saying that my journey has been about instilling hope and about preserving, protecting, and promoting what makes the health service and a career in medicine in particular so special. As I returned to full-time clinical practice, I found that vision became even more important, and I feel that the experiences of medical politics actually made me a better clinician – I now listen more.

Commentary

As we read Krishna's account, we can't help but feel for him as he relates the experience and discomfort of being a fish out of water, a compassionate leader at home in general practice who is learning to swim in shark-infested waters. We might accept and even applaud his efforts, but the easy thing would be to say 'politics is not for me' and skim over what he has to say. That would be a shame and a lost opportunity, because Krishna holds up a mirror in which we can see reflected the politics and tribalism that are a part of many leaders' lives, whether we work with a political organisation or not.

So how is this relevant to all of us? Krishna describes joining a political community that negotiates on behalf of its members about their livelihoods and their terms and conditions of work. Such negotiations are critically important. We can't pretend that we don't need politics or that we don't need courageous people to step up and represent us.

Is that your view? How do you feel about colleagues who sit, for example, on committees. Do you feel supportive or regret their absence from clinical work? Maybe you feel suspicious of the value of their work or even their motives?

In practice life, we have 'political' encounters as we too, have high-stakes negotiations with people who have power and maybe can harm us if we get it wrong. Negotiations between doctors as employers and their employees are an example of this. Also, leaders who find themselves in positions of greater influence may not have gone into politics but will find politics coming to them as a natural dimension of their work.

We get an insight from Krishna about the nature of this political dimension, what it demands, what it feels like, and the challenges it creates. Politics shows this in stark form, but the lessons from Krishna's world can be applied wherever we find ourselves transacting with the powerful.

He describes moving from the value-base of a caring profession to a quite different tribe with its own values and ways of working. Krishna finds himself in an uncomfortable no man's land of wanting to be true to the values of those he represents whilst trying to be effective on their behalf with people who can't be trusted in ways he is used to. Perhaps this is because their values are different or poorly understood.

Does this resonate with you? Have you experienced the 'norming' pressure of joining an organisation and having to adopt their values and ways of working?

How did you avoid selling out on those important things that you weren't comfortable with?

In negotiations that are high-stakes, people often wish to get their way, avoid being harmed, and retain the confidence of those they represent. Is this ever possible? This is not the arena for being reasonable, hearing different perspectives and being willing to shift. If we did those things, they might be interpreted by the other side and by our own communities as being 'weakness' or capitulation. Therefore, arguments get simplified, people are categorised as either us or them, and positions become both polarised and entrenched.

Look at the last sentence. Are these approaches a bad thing? You may have done any or all of these things. If so, how do you justify that, and in what circumstances would you do so again?

In clinical life, compassion, openness, and honesty are underlined. In politics, they are underused. Political communities may use power to assert and enforce whereas clinical communities will use influence to relate and adapt. Each community has the capacity to change the other, and this insight can help us in a number of ways.

Firstly, we can recall the old adage 'power corrupts' and remember that our attitudes, ambitions, and behaviours are at risk if we become too enmeshed.

Good people can become damaged by power; it doesn't just happen to others. What do you think the dangerous lures of power might be? Which of these might you personally be susceptible to, and which have you given in to in the past?

Krishna relates his discomfort, and, although we might feel sympathy for him, we might also feel pleased or even relieved that he still has this feeling. Discomfort at the influence of power on our attitudes and behaviour is a sign that we haven't been completely drawn in and become unquestioning. We can't avoid the exercise of power as it comes with the territory, but as leaders we can remember Krishna's example, hold on to our discomfort, and protect ourselves from forgetting our purpose.

Leaders working in a political dimension usually step out of their comfort zone and do an unenviable job on behalf of others. They need to keep their discomfort alive, but they also need understanding and compassion.

Most of us are colleagues of people like this, so what would you do to address these needs? Such people may be unlikely to ask for our assistance, so how could you help them to survive, grow, and also know when to quit?

We noted above that a political environment can challenge clinical communities and their relationship-based values like openness and inclusion. However, the reverse in which clinical culture influences political behaviour is not only possible but, we feel, necessary. As more clinicians become active in situations of power, they have the choice to resist assimilation or corruption, and instead enrich the political work in a couple of significant ways.

Firstly, bringing in a problem-solving mindset rather than a confrontational one is much better suited to analysing and working through complex problems. All significant issues, including those with political dimensions, are complex by nature. To oversimplify and adopt the solutions put forward by the most powerful denies the reality of complexity and may be counterproductive. We are not saying that the traditional political methods are wrong, more that they are not always appropriate or sufficient.

Secondly, the approaches of compassionate leaders foster the ability of people to listen, understand, and value each other in ways that make collaboration much more fruitful. Again, there is a place for the tradition of polarising people and perspectives, especially when urgent decisions and actions are needed. However, every issue has phases in which collaboration is needed in order to think and act more effectively. Once again, we see how methods are not intrinsically good or bad, but are more or less *effective* in bringing about useful change. Our task is to lay assumptions and prejudice to one side and use the right tools for the circumstance.

You may not agree with the morally neutral stance taken above. If so, why do you feel uncomfortable?

Political dialogue doesn't encourage this, but a powerful part of connecting better with people is by showing our vulnerability. For example, in a meeting we might admit that we don't know something or that we feel confused or need help to understand the feelings in the room. These need not be seen as signs of weakness, but we should also take care to be sincere in our actions and not to seek to manipulate others through our behaviour. In other settings, putting something of our own doubts and fears on the table humanises us and is usually appreciated by others. We would be wise not to be naïve and also keep vigilant for signs of being taken advantage of. However, it is only by trying, failing, and trying again that new and more helpful norms can be established. *Especially* when things have never been different, that doesn't mean they never can be.

Krishna muses on political careers ending in failure and suggests that maybe we should not see such work as a career. Trying to do the right thing at the time may be the most valid measure of our success as history, which rarely has access to the truth of the circumstances, may paint our efforts unfairly. Knowing that may help us to sustain and survive.

We've seen here how Krishna's reflections have meaning and relevance for us all. Just as in his own work, there are always higher stakes and more confrontational situations in which we have to engage with people and find a way forward.

How would you gauge whether your own time working with political issues was worthwhile? How would you know when to hand over?

What we've seen is that politics and politicians are not the enemy; they have approaches we can learn about and learn from.

We need them because they grapple with some of the most critical issues that affect our survival. However, when we engage with politics, as we need to, we can enrich what it is capable of rather than becoming corrupted. If we keep up the dialogue with our community, particularly with those we trust, we can use their feedback to keep our discomfort alive, avoid selling out, and pick up on signs that we need to move on.

In this way we, and those who follow, can change the system for the better. Our political work therefore does not end in failure with a hot potato being dropped, but with a baton being handed on to the next person who is courageous enough to accept the challenge it represents. In your community, who might that be?

Further reading from *The Leadership Hike*

Chapter 1 on shifting the organisational culture.
Chapter 6 on listening to ourselves and not trying to fit in.
Chapter 16 on adapting and surviving in difficult situations.
Chapter 25 on retaining your values in the face of pressure.

Podcast with the author

In this podcast, Krishna Kasaraneni describes how he became interested in leadership and how he was inspired to take up leadership roles, including being a member of the BMA's General Practice Committee, and discusses:

- His inspiration to take on a leadership role and the challenges of medical politics.
- Managing situations in which people have strong convictions and equally strong disagreements.
- Being as open as you can be in sensitive situations, including doing things that are not popular, but necessary.

CHAPTER

12

Austin O'Carroll

Austin O'Carroll is a GP in Dublin, the founder of the North Dublin GP training scheme and also the founder of Safetynet, The Granby Clinic, and GP Care for all, all specialising in providing care for marginalised people, many struggling with homelessness and addiction. He was awarded WONCA Europe GP of the year in 2020.

At my age, all stories start long, long ago as does that of my leadership journey. I was born with severe disabilities due to the drug thalidomide. I had multiple surgeries before I could walk at aged 5. Between the ages of 5 and 13, I visited the doctor annually to assess whether I required further intervention. Each of those seven visits resulted in further planned surgery. Each recovery required learning to walk again and then learning to run again so I could play with my friends. Inevitably, each recovery came to a jarring crash as I returned to the operating table. I learnt two lessons during this period. Firstly, to expect failure. It was easier to visit the surgeon's beautiful mahogany- and leather-filled office expecting bad news than having hopes repeatedly dashed. If you prepare for failure, you become liberated from fear of failure. Secondly, I learnt about persistence – the attribute that gave me the gift of walking. Persistence was a gift that I have exploited, in all aspects of my life: professional, familial, romantic, and parental.

DOI: 10.1201/ 9781003270492-13

EXAMPLE OF PERSISTENCE	
Intermediate Care Centre	In 2005, local hospitals were discharging homeless patients who were well enough to be nursed at 'home', but 'homeless' hostels were ill-equipped to provide effective care. Many ended up being re-admitted shortly after discharge. There were also patients too unwell to be cared for in hostels but who were not sick enough for hospital admission. Along with two colleagues, I approached the Health Service Executive (HSE), who commissioned a report outlining the arguments for and against developing an intermediate care/step-up step-down facility, which existed in the United States. We made two arguments. Firstly, it was the right thing to do for homeless people; secondly, it was cost-effective as it prevented costly hospital (re)admissions. The HSE initially agreed to fund the initiative. Unfortunately, the funding was due to be finalised when the 2007 worldwide recession hit. The funding was withdrawn. Every year, I re-submitted the proposal. I persistently promoted the concept and the evidence base supporting its development. Eventually in 2018 the funding was obtained, and Dublin Simon opened a step-up/step-down (intermediate) care centre with Safetynet.

I was the youngest of six children. My childhood was happy, particularly our heated discussions over dinner. We argued for hours over political, religious, and social issues. My mother was particularly conservative and often ended up being a lone voice. To ensure the discussions continued, we took turns to argue her point of view. Interestingly, this taught me the skills of adopting another's perspective. Leaders need to understand the perspectives of others, including those on one's own team who have differing views or approaches and those outside the team whom you need to recruit, ally with, persuade, or challenge in order to achieve further your team goals.

EXAMPLE OF UNDERSTANDING ANOTHER'S PERSPECTIVE	
Working with the Health Services Executive (HSE)	I have worked with the HSE for many years. Initially, if I found a gap in service provision, I would point out the system's failure. Occasionally, I used the public media to make my argument. I quickly found out that rather than holding their hands up and accepting the truth of my observations, the HSE would adopt a defensive position. On reflection, I realised that the HSE is criticised on a weekly basis in the media. It is a huge organisation, with multiple services. Medical and organisational mishaps were inevitable, often ending up in the public press. The barrage of criticism without recognition of the vast amount of positive work they did was morale-sapping for staff. It was no surprise they became defensive. Since that realisation, I have sought partnership with the HSE and always presented issues as opportunities to plug gaps rather than criticisms. I have always given praise for the vast amount of successes they have and the fantastic services they provide, and we have collaborated on many successful projects.

At 20 years, I entered the leafy glades of Trinity College Dublin. I received two educations in this eminent institution: one inside the walls in medical labs and lecture halls and the other outside those walls in streets, playgrounds, and alleys of inner-city Dublin. Though an agnostic, I worked with the Vincent de Paul [(England & Wales) is part of an international Christian voluntary network dedicated to tackling poverty] visiting old folks and running youth projects in the corporation flats that housed those descended from the tenements of Dublin. Academia gave me knowledge and professional skills. Charitable work gave me a love and empathy for those enduring the poverty of Dublin. This equipped me with a passion and drive to work in areas of deprivation. I also learned the direction I wanted to travel. It was not a Google Maps route with a clear outline of where to go, but rather a compass bearing. I knew I wanted to head North.

EXAMPLE OF KNOWING COMPASS BEARING	
North Dublin City GP Training Programme	I loved teaching and was working as an assistant programme director on a training scheme that focused on training high-quality GPs. However, it did not clearly align with the direction I was travelling as it did not clearly address health inequity. On reflection I realised that though people in areas of deprivation and those from marginalised communities had the worst health indices by a clear mile, as per Tudor Hart's inverse care law they had the poorest access to health services including general practice. That is when I came up with the idea of developing a GP training scheme that focused on training GPs to work with these communities. As we worked towards launching the scheme, many colleagues advised not to advertise the focus of the scheme as they worried there would be few applicants. On consideration, I decided we should advertise the focus on deprivation and marginalisation. This would ensure those applying would be committed to the focus on equity. Surprisingly, since its launch the scheme has had the highest number of applications per training place in Ireland. We should not have been surprised that young people did seek to address inequity.

In medical school, I worked as a summer project coordinator providing entertainment over an 8-week period for over 1000 inner-city children. I worked with a committee of local people and 18 local volunteers. Two of those volunteers were particularly unreliable and lazy. I asked them to run a tennis competition. Despite numerous meetings to support them, they did not sign up a single child. Eventually, I decided to run the competition and signed up 50 children. That night an emergency committee meeting was called in which the two volunteers complained about me taking over the competition. I explained my case. I received no support. I realised I had two choices: resign or apologise. With gritted teeth, I apologised. After the meeting, many committee members apologised saying they believed I was right, but they could not support me over a local person. My brothers and sisters were furious and advised me to resign immediately. I did not resign. This taught me that you sometimes have to take some unjust hits on the chin if you want something strongly enough. Keeping a clear eye on my primary objective helped me not take offence.

Motivation

EXAMPLE OF NOT TAKING OFFENCE AND KEEPING AN EYE ON THE DESIRED OUTCOME	
Clinical Lead for Covid Homeless Response	I was appointed clinical lead for the Covid Homeless Response. Prior to this appointment, a vast number of organisations and individuals had been arranging meetings and initiating interventions. Bringing all this positive energy involved negotiating between and assigning clear roles/responsibilities to differing organisations. This inevitably caused friction, and I experienced vigorous disputes and complaints including receiving personal criticism. It was important not to react to the criticism personally but to either work out a positive consensus or, if required, make decisions that left some feeling left down and then rebuild those relationships. Not taking offence and keeping an eye on the desired outcome was critical to ensuring this vast team worked efficiently together.

Over the years, I developed philosophical perspectives which moulded my approach to addressing marginalisation. As a leader, one of my roles was to foster these philosophies in the teams I worked with.

- In the mid-1990s, I joined a disability rights advocacy group called Forum of the People of Disabilities. They introduced me to the human rights–based approach to inequity. I still have a huge respect for the motivation of people who are involved in charitable endeavours. I now believe that charity is not a transformative approach to inequity. It does not challenge the societal structures that create and maintain inequity.
- The concept of the structural determinants of health delineates how health is not simply dependent on 'healthy living' and having a good doctor but on a wide spectrum of social factors including poverty, education, employment, housing, community, and environment. This approach offered a framework to gather evidence in support of the social influences on health so evident in my inner-city practice.
- When I discovered trauma-informed care, it felt I had found a philosophical home. This theory arose from the evidence that exposure to childhood trauma results in a vast range of negative health and

social outcomes including lower life expectancy, poorer physical and mental health, higher risk of involvement in substance misuse, crime, violence, and higher likelihood of engaging in poor health behaviours. This theory in particular spoke to the care of many of my own patients who were homeless, engaged in substance misuse, and/or displayed challenging behaviours. Trauma-informed care encourages service providers to engage with clients in ways that do not end up repeating the trauma. It views substance misuse as self-treatment of the pain caused by childhood trauma and its sequelae.

BENEFITS OF HAVING A CLEAR PHILOSOPHY	
Policy on Managing Challenging Behaviours	In 1997, I took over a single-handed GP practice in inner-city Dublin. It was shocking to witness how devastated this community was by poverty and addiction. I met so many young men and women caught up in the maelstrom of chaos of drugs and alcohol. I attended so many funerals of young people. I met so many parents who had lost one, two, three, or four children due to substance misuse. I met so many homeless people. I met so many people who had so little hope of a worthwhile future or long life span. I have always taught my staff to manage behaviours using a non-confrontational approach. We believe most of our clients as children had rules enforced with stick, fist, or shouting. When we apply rules strictly we evoke responses clients learnt as children. We talk clients down, take them outside, crack a joke, reason with them, get them to return later. The aim is to maintain the relationship. On the rare occasions we bar someone; it is usually temporary and we refer to a fellow agency to manage them in the interim. This approach has been solidified by training all staff in trauma-informed care. Interestingly, this approach improves staff morale as they can feel empathy for difficult clients.

I had been introduced to the concept of vision and mission when working in the disability movement. Vision is the way you would like the world to be, and mission is how you will contribute to achieving that vision. When a vision and mission spring out of a genuine passion, they transform from a potential paper exercise to a vital, energising, and compelling dynamic that fuels one's motivation towards a defined goal.

EXAMPLES OF WHERE VISION AND MISSION EMPOWERED AND INSPIRED THE TEAM	
North Dublin GP Training Scheme (NDCGP)	On the very first week of the NDCGP, the two programme directors (Dr Ming Rawat and I) and trainees sat together and devised a vision and mission. Our original vision was 'Every person in Ireland has access to the highest quality and professional GP services', and our original mission was 'To educate GPs who have the expertise and passion to maximise patients health irrespective of background and whose own health is maximised through the ability to self-care'. Every year we re-visit the vision and mission. From 2014 Fiona O Reilly helped the trainees to set up a V&M Committee whose focus was to make the vision and mission real through action. In their first year, they organised the first Irish Street Medicine Conference which has now become an annual event attended by 100–200 health providers to marginalised communities. In their second year, they decided to take a theme from the vision and mission for each year and chose the theme of access. They then set up two new GP trainee–run clinics: one for undocumented migrants (the first of its kind) and one in a hostel for homeless people. In their third year they chose advocacy and ran a campaign for better treatment of asylum seekers. In their fourth year they chose quality and reviewed GP services for homeless people the scheme was involved in to ensure they were equipped to a high-quality standard and so on. This constant re-visiting of the vision and mission has ensured that they continue to inspire each subsequent generation of trainees.

The creation of a persuasive argument for introducing a change is a necessary skill for those seeking to develop service responses. In 2015 I completed a professional doctorate in health in 2015 on homeless people's use of health services. A doctorate equips you with the skills to create persuasive evidence-based arguments. It also means you become a world expert in your area of research. This expertise means that people are more likely to listen to your arguments and consider your proposals. Leadership is not static. It requires growth and development.

PRODUCING EVIDENCE-BASED ARGUMENTS	
Stabilisation Centre for Rough Sleepers	I have been doing outreach on the streets since 2005. There are a number of factors that contribute to people's decision to sleep rough, including mental illness, drug and/or alcohol addiction, or fear of aggression in hostels. It became apparent that a simple offer of accommodation for rough sleepers was often not enough to persuade them to leave the streets. One needed to provide a package of care that would address all their needs. I conducted a literature review on addiction and rough sleeping and a needs analysis by talking to rough sleepers on the street. I presented the findings of this to the health and housing authorities and proposed a rough sleeper stabilisation centre that would allow them stabilise their substance misuse and enable them to move into an appropriate accommodation. It was launched in April 2022.

I manage a large community GP practice: a large GP and addiction practice for homeless people, a GP training scheme, a GP service for four stabilisation/detox centres, and a GP service for asylum seekers. This requires, firstly, recruiting the right people. Critically, we prioritised those who were attracted to the practice vision and mission. Secondly, we recruited people whose particular skills and strengths would add to the team skill set and so add to the overall team potential.

Once I have a team in place, I have two tasks. Firstly, I must keep the team focused on the vision and mission and, secondly, ensure the team has the support and leadership to work effectively. I love sailing. In racing, the captain of the boat has to ensure, firstly, that their boat is set up so it can go as fast as possible. Secondly, they have to ensure their crew work effectively together, encouraging them to take initiative and constantly sharing information and opinions to reach decisions by consensus when possible, while knowing on rare occasions the captain has to make a decision and the crew need to respect that decision. Once sailing effectively, the captain and crew need to observe the weather and tide conditions so as to plot the fastest course. Lastly, once all these issues have been addressed, they need to observe what their competitors are doing. If a boat and crew is set up correctly, then the captain needs only keep a light hand on the tiller as the boat will sail itself. I find this analogy is useful for team development.

A leader also needs to learn the skills of persuading others to support and fund projects. My GP trainer introduced me to the black-and-white film *12 Angry Men* (1957), which she described as a masterpiece on the art of persuasion. I learnt two very valuable lessons from that film. Firstly, knowing when to do a hard sell and when to do a soft sell. Hard sells involve pressurising the person to make the decision you want now. It can involve loading them with information as to why they should do what you want them to do, creating a sense of urgency as to why this must be done now, and just hard neck and persistence. Hard sells are useful when you need something done urgently, when you have only a short window of opportunity, and/or when the evidence or arguments for taking action are really clear and obvious. The danger of a hard sell is the person who is the victim of the hard sell can feel hurried and 'used'. The soft sell is an approach of gentle persuasion, which often starts with a request not to take an action but to discuss the possibility of taking an action. A soft sell may involve phrases such as 'I am only asking you to look at this, not to make a decision' or 'All I am asking is you read this'. Soft sells usually involve relationship building. Since viewing that film, I have always considered which would be the better approach, a hard or soft sell. This requires reflectivity in action.[1] The second nugget I gained from that film was about the futility of seeking to persuade those whose opinion will not change. This resonates with the concept of early adopters versus laggards as outlined in *The Leadership Hike*. Since that film, I have never expended energy on seeking to persuade those who are unpersuadable. I look to more reasonable people to listen to my arguments and politely decline to give those who are rigid in their view a platform to expound them. These are concepts that actually are explored thoroughly in change management theory, which is well outlined in *The Leadership Hike*.

EXAMPLE OF ALLIANCE BUILDING	
Safetynet Mobile Health Unit (MHU) for Rough Sleepers	One day I received an offer of a decommissioned mobile surgery. I immediately accepted. I talked to the HSE about using this to provide mobile health services to rough sleepers. They were not only not interested, but actively objected. They felt such a service was retrograde. So I approached the four Dublin GP training schemes and suggested that GP trainees could provide an out-of-hours service 2 nights a week using this unit. I argued it would help them achieve their mandatory out-of-hours commitment while also enabling them to develop skills and challenge any attitudes they had in working with homeless people. I simultaneously recruited a number of volunteer GPs to work as supervisors. Lastly, I approached the Dublin Simon Rough Sleeper Team and suggested if they worked with the MHU, both services could mutually enhance each other. Everyone agreed, and we launched the MHU in 2009. Research we conducted in 2013 confirmed that GP trainees found the service challenged their preconceptions of homeless people positively and that the majority of rough sleepers using the service said they would not have accessed any other service. Over the years many rough sleepers who had refused to connect with the Simon Rough Sleeper team had got to know them while awaiting the doctor. Several of these who had been rough sleeping for years were persuaded to move into accommodation. After 10 years, the HSE recognised the value of the MHU and agreed to fund a nurse to support the trainees. This whole process required the use of the full range of change management skills.

In this story of leadership, I have left out a very important chapter, that of the failings I have as a leader and the mistakes I made along the road. The failings are many: some I have learnt to iron out, and some are integral to my personality. I have always liked initiating projects. I was poor at project maintenance skills. I had the energy and passion to establish services but lacked interest in the governance and administrative tasks required to ensure an organisation survived. Hence, I recruited people to the team who had these skills. However, I became aware I could frustrate such valuable team members. I have always had too many projects on the go, juggling too many balls. Many balls came crashing to the ground due to me losing concentration or becoming exhausted. It is no accident my team called me Dr Chaos. I needed to address these deficits. The arts of reflectivity and acceptance (and seeking) of feedback are essential, as one cannot address a factor that one is not aware of. Once identified, I addressed these factors either by seeking to learn skills (e.g., how to develop governance structures, how to have systems for addressing detail, and how to keep a proper diary) or by knowing when to let leadership go (i.e., either share the leadership role with someone who has the necessary attributes or leave entirely and let the organisation thrive without being constrained by the founder syndrome). Founder syndrome is where a founder stays on too long, and as founders tend to be strong personalities, they can inhibit the necessary evolution of the project/team.

What have I learnt along this voyage? Firstly, leaders are not born; they develop. Anyone can learn to be a leader. Secondly, leadership requires having a clear vision and mission. Lastly, leadership requires constant reflectivity on one's actions, on one's strengths and deficits, and how to augment strengths and diminish deficits. I have so enjoyed this journey. I have loved meeting the many amazing people who have travelled the road with me. I have been saddened by the failures we have encountered along the way. But I also have enjoyed the successes. Boy, have I enjoyed those successes!

Commentary

We are all shaped by our experiences: they influence how we think, respond, and behave both as human beings and as leaders. The challenge Austin O'Carroll faced by growing up with, living with, and achieving professionally with considerable physical disability seems significant. Recognising his vulnerability, he prepared himself for failure during his own medical interventions, such that in adulthood he no longer feared failure. Fear of failure is a common human trait that gets in the way of us trying new things or feeling able to influence services and organisations. We see signs of this when we procrastinate or hold ourselves back from sharing ideas, and it can manifest as perfectionism. We often fear being judged as being 'not enough' such that it can be easier to keep our heads below the parapet. Not fearing failure must surely be a super power for a leader. If we consider 'What's the worst thing that can happen?' and know we will be able to handle it, it means very little will stand in the way of us having a go. Changing our belief around what constitutes success or failure can reduce anxiety we may feel around taking action. Giving up a tendency to binary thinking (that our work either succeeds or fails) helps us to reflect and learn as we act, meaning that all results generate learning regardless of traditional measures of success. Effective leadership often needs us to have the courage to take risks and to persist in trying to achieve a goal, even when things are difficult. It takes courage to show our vulnerability and share when we don't know the answer or the way forward. These attitudes and behaviours can in turn inspire others to let go of their fears and pursue a course of action without knowing if it will achieve the intended goal.

It seems useful to think about how our own fear of failure might impact how we behave in our organisations. It may be that this trait causes us to suppress the ideas or enthusiasm of others if we are held back by our anxieties around failure. If this is a tendency you recognise in yourself, how might you test out letting go of this habit and allow others to run with their ideas even when you feel failure is inevitable?

Austin recognises his childhood experiences with surgery led him to expect failure and to not be afraid of it. Despite this, he has hung on to his optimism, which seems unusual. Are you aware of how experiences from your past have shaped your current responses to situations and leadership choices? How might you change these responses if they aren't serving you well?

In most of Austin's work streams he has shown courage and persistence. The root of some of this courage seems to have emerged from the expectation of disappointment from his childhood surgical procedures. It may also reflect his actions being motivated by a clear vision, rather than necessarily by external measures of success or failure. Though he was traumatised from the outset by forces beyond his control, rather than feeling victimised he found another way to use this powerful force. He developed a deep empathy and compassion for the vulnerable and the marginalised and an understanding of the value of advocacy for people who struggle to advocate for themselves. His experiences helped to shape his vision and mission.

Leaders with such a strong sense of mission who don't allow initial lack of success to get in their way can seem unstoppable. He seems highly aware of what drives and motivates him and talks of how his vision emerged and the work he does to establish and regularly revisit the vision and mission within the organisations he leads. Effective leadership starts with an awareness of self. Our ability to persist in the face of setbacks is highly dependent on whether the work we do is in tune with our personal drives as well as our attitude towards notions of success and failure. Though organisations can strive to establish a shared vision and mission, it may be unreasonable to expect all members of a team to have the same drive and motivation.

It can be useful to consider the impact of this in your organisation. If you find yourself in a position of working with others who are motivated differently from you, how might you respond?

How might a strong vision and pursuit of a goal come across as lack of flexibility? Others may interpret persistence as getting in the way of collaboration and consensus building. How might you navigate having a clear vision and goal whilst also actively participating in co-production?

Austin has achieved significant gains for the population he serves, and we are interested to explore the sources of his power. Business and organisation experts have researched and theorised on sources of personal power and how these can be used by leaders to get things done. We all have power and need to make choices about how we use it. Quite early in Austin's journey, he made use of 'expert power' to help him achieve his goal of setting up an intermediate care facility for homeless patients in Dublin. Demonstrating expert knowledge, in this case by a presentation of the evidence base for an intervention or new service, can be a powerful force when working with systems. System leaders, especially those who are in control of the distribution of limited resources, can feel comforted by expertise when making decisions. Expertise augments our power, but it can be tempting to misuse this power. Acquiring subject knowledge can lead us to a belief that we can be more certain about a course of action. However, as Einstein is quoted, 'The more I learn, the more I realise I don't know'. This reflects how the deeper we understand a subject area, the more we recognise the subtleties, the nuance, and the areas of uncertainty. How certain can we be that our ideas and plans will achieve the outcome we want, even if the evidence suggests it will? The evidence may not have been gathered in the same context, and the variables and confounding factors may mean we have a dilemma about whether to present the evidence with the level of certainty that might satisfy the commissioners of services, or whether we are honest about our uncertainty.

The completion of his PhD in the experiences of homeless people when accessing healthcare will have significantly deepened his expert power. No longer does the expertise lie in the evidence-based documents, but in the person, augmented by empathy and lived experience, and this will strengthen his ability to influence others. Like every source of power, we need to use it with consideration. The greater our expert power, the greater the temptation to use it to compel others rather than to persuade them to our way of thinking.

Austin's recognition of the shadow side of power comes out clearly in his decision to step away from Safetynet, the charity he had co-founded. Founders of organisations carry a certain specific positional power that has often been seen to stifle the growth and development of the organisation once it has been established and is running well. As the person who 'gave birth' to the organisation, their views on its future can be perceived as carrying more weight than the views of others and it can be much harder for the founder to 'let go' of the future direction.

Think about your sources of power. Are you putting your power to good use and aware of when overusing this power may cause harm?

Austin's recognition of the potential for 'founder's syndrome' and the action taken is a demonstration of reflexivity. When we lead, we make a series of choices about how we act and interact with others. Reflexive leaders are then aware of the outcome of the choice they make and learn from this, which then guides future choices. The ability to not only be part of a situation, but also to observe the situation at the same time, watching for the subtleties and the impact of your choices, is a skill that takes practice. It requires a high level of self-awareness to, at times, halt our gut reaction to give time to consider the impact of this reaction on others. It seems that watching the well-crafted film *12 Angry Men* was akin to a light-bulb moment for Austin. He saw how the skills of reading a room, watching the responses of others, and adapting an approach 'in the moment' could lead to a positive outcome. Pausing to consider the best approach and making a choice is not something that comes naturally to many of us, but it is a very useful leadership skill and can be learned and practiced.

Think about the last meeting you were part of and what choices you made during the interactions. Were there things you decided not to say because you decided there might be a better way of achieving a better outcome?

Further reading from *The Leadership Hike*

Chapter 7 on understanding and working with our limitations.
Chapter 17 for how to establish a clear, shared vision and direction for your organisation.
Chapter 19 for how to create buy-in and facilitate consensus.
Chapter 24 for how we can use our influence at a system level.

Podcast with the author

In this podcast, Austin O'Connell shares his thoughts on:

- How leaders can use anger or a feeling of injustice to drive them to make a difference.
- How to gather others around you to lead better, as everyone brings something different.
- The importance of a clear vision and mission.

Note

1 Reflectivity in action is the ability to reflect on one's actions in real time. It is a skill that can be developed by reflecting 'on action' (i.e., reflecting on one's performance after the event has taken place). Persistent reflection on action allows one become aware of how one acts and so enables them to identify these patterns of behaviour when they happen in action and thus gives them choice whether to behave in that or another way.

CHAPTER

13

Owen Richards

Over a long career in the management and commissioning services in the NHS, Owen has sought ways to listen and respond to the voices of local people. These methods have included working with representative bodies such as community health councils and also involving local residents in the design and evaluation of services.

Owen has represented patients nationally, bringing their voices to the RCGP and the Academy of Medical Royal Colleges. In both roles, he has tried to improve the system through sharing the experience and perspectives of real people.

Graduate training schemes often evoke a degree of cynicism amongst the established workforce – here he comes, still wet behind the ears, fresh out of university. Yes, that was me. In the 1980s, when I joined the NHS management training scheme, I started with a Cook's tour – a day in the laundry, as a domestic cleaning toilets on the ward. I got bawled out of theatres by an orthopaedic consultant because no one had asked his permission for me to observe. A community mental health nurse planned a brilliant day – starting with a client in a small flat, sticky carpets, piles of rubbish everywhere. 'He'll offer you a cup of tea. Your choice'.

In a hospital for people with learning disabilities, I was given a passkey, with the freedom and power to enter and leave the villas; it was a distinctly uncomfortable feeling. One young woman, deaf as a consequence of boxing her own ears, with poor sight, sensed me and wrapped my arms around her waist just for comfort, I guess. Every lunchtime, on my way to the staff canteen, I was propositioned by a lady: 'Will you marry me? And take me home?'

DOI: 10.1201/ 9781003270492-14

There I was, a couple of decades later, in front of an audience of some 500 people including the MP and all the borough councillors, trying to persuade them that closing a community hospital, with its under-utilised minor injuries unit, and some care of the elderly beds was 'a good thing'. The audience didn't seem to understand why our plans made so much sense to us – what was wrong with my presentation? I then got 'volunteered' to go on local radio, trying to justify withdrawing a certain novel chemotherapy drug. I put forward the usual sort of things we say when money is tight and we need to 'transform care' using evidence. 'Hello caller – do you want to put your question to Owen?' I heard her tell me and the whole world how this particular drug had given her extra time with her grandchildren, how that could not be measured in monetary terms. All I could do was to apologise and mumble something about the evidence base and wait for the ground to swallow me up. Dear reader, it never does.

Feet up. Glass of whisky in my hand. What can I reflect on?

I saw care and compassion in shovel loads everywhere. I was in a position of privilege: to work with clinicians, to be allowed into patients' homes and hear their stories, and to gain insight from which I could draw in the future. This early experience affirmed my desire to collaborate with caregivers to enable them to deliver the services patients needed.

A clinical career was not for me, but I was influenced by my family's public service ethos. Teachers sought to improve life chances, ministers of religion comforted, and my father, a civil servant, supported farmers and fishermen to supply the country with food. I thought I could support clinicians to deliver high-quality healthcare. Also, my parents were getting older – how did I want them to be treated? How would I want to be cared for?

Towards the end of my NHS career, I felt removed from those who I had originally joined the NHS to serve – the patients. Was me sitting in an office in London as a regulator or working on grant allocations really making a difference? Sitting in a community centre, chairing a grants panel, having real conversations about life in that parish or village made my work more meaningful, especially if challenged by other trustees who were not party to those conversations. For me, it reinforced the need to work with people, as equals. One fellow trustee talked about 'amplifying voices' – that was me, an amplifier, talking to individuals and groups about their experiences of health and social care and using their stories when I met with local leaders.

Apart from realising that the ground never opens up, what else have I learned?

Hindsight is a wonderful thing, and here are some reflections on my hike through the NHS.

What's a leader?

One definition of leadership is 'the ability and capacity to lead and influence others, by means of personal attributes and/or behaviours, to achieve a common goal'. Clinicians, managers, and support staff all share the common goal of making people better and keeping them healthy. We all share a goal of 'do no harm'. I developed a standard interview answer when asked about risk-taking as a manager: fine, provided no patients are harmed and I don't squander public money (in that order). Having that at my core connects me better to clinicians somehow – surely managers are only interested in money and targets? I hope that when I am in the room, I bring constructive challenge on behalf of the people I represent, those whose voices are not in the room. I listen, I try to find ways of unblocking problems, I share positive feedback, I empathise. None of these is peculiar to managers or leaders. Let's also not forget that patients can be leaders too: they seek to influence by telling their own stories to help that 'common goal'; they may also bring history and community intelligence to the room – what has been tried previously and ought not to be forgotten. So let's have co-chairs of redesign groups, with proper support and investment.

Do clinicians understand why patient experience is important?

It seems an odd question to ask. No one wants a patient to have a bad experience. Is this where art and science need to come together? Much of clinical practice appears to revolve around quantitative changes – weight gain/loss, increase/decrease in depression scales, or changes in INR. Even considering 'patient activation' comes with a score. Does this lead to less consideration being given to subjective issues, such as how a patient felt about an intervention or episode? However, we also know that good experiences mean that patients will engage with screening and vaccination programmes and comply better with treatment. With an increased role for primary care in population health management, and in influencing pathways, leaders need to consider how they work with partners to capture a broader sweep of patient experience and bring more patients and carers into the co-design of services. Meaningful engagement also helps patients grow in autonomy and confidence, in turn bringing greater well-being.

Getting it wrong

A lesson in learning about outcomes came from that classic moment when as a manager I challenged a clinician about an element of practice. 'Your referrals to orthopaedics are really high compared to neighbouring practices, aren't they?' There was a sigh, a slight shake of the head. 'Sonny, have you looked at the conversion rates? The number of my patients who go on to surgery, compared to other practices?' So despite my early wish to 'do the right thing', I had failed to look at the whole patient experience. Meetings after that were different – and we had constructive conversations. You too will get it wrong, that first engagement event you run. Reflect and do it again.

> Ever tried. Ever failed. No matter. Try again. Fail again. Fail better.
>
> **(Samuel Beckett)**

Patient stories are really powerful

In the early days of the commissioner/provider split, writing commissioning intentions from my ivory tower was so easy. We ran presentations for local GPs, but we never talked to those who needed the services we planned. One of the services covered by the process was in vitro fertilisation. Couples failing to meet our criteria would call, struggling to manage their emotions. Hardest of all was being asked if I had children. It brought home the impact of my actions on individual lives, the lives we never encountered from our offices.

With more reflection, the next time I spoke to that borough council about a structural change in the NHS locally, I went along with Ethel, an imaginary local resident. You all know her: she's elderly, alone, with a couple of long-term conditions and in poor housing. Suddenly, all my customary NHS-speak disappeared and the elected members really understood what I was asking them to support.

Language is critical

Spoken and unspoken. Clinicians and managers can all too easily fall into the bear trap of using jargon. Speak plainly, use simple words, but do not patronise. Spell out the acronym several times and think, 'How would I explain this to a friend who works outside the NHS?'

At one event a lady with arthritis spoke about how her preferred outcome from treatment was to be able to make a Christmas cake with her granddaughter. She understood why biomarkers were important in monitoring her condition but did not want to be just a number. Referring to Mrs Khan as a person with diabetes rather than a diabetic isn't part of the woke culture; you are recognising her as a real person. She exists: Her Hb_{A1c} results are not what define her.

The day after that large public meeting, a colleague took me to one side and carefully pointed out how my body language had spoken volumes about my impatience with the audience and how it unwittingly created a barrier between me and the people I needed to win over. I was shocked and, if I am honest, a little hurt.

The amateur interest in medicine did help *me* learn another language: the ability to not look flustered when a medical term was used in a conversation amongst clinicians assisted in building relationships. Think about how you might learn the languages of those you work with and for.

Set the context

I once spoke at a local council's community panel. 'We need more GPs', the public and councillors said. 'Why don't you just appoint them?' With a GP supporting me, we talked about how general practice is funded and operates. There was surprise that GPs were not NHS employees, that their business model was not dissimilar to other professionals. We spoke about how each time a planning authority gave consent for a new housing development, it was creating pressure on all public services. A partnership between local residents, their councillors, and the NHS was critical to health and well-being. Our aim at that session was to help residents understand how this Byzantine thing called the NHS really worked, so that future conversations became more mature. Knowledge was power, but we willingly shared it. How can we expect residents to work with us if they can only see part of the jigsaw puzzle? As a manager, I could just have used the same old jargon and excuses. It took some of my leadership to listen actively, reflect, support the room, and paint a picture of how we could work together

Not long afterwards, a large audience assembled at a planning committee to register concerns about a hostel for people with mental health issues, planned for a residential area. I was a coopted member of that committee, to give a health perspective on applications. I could have simply referenced the government targets. Instead, I spoke about the sorts of individuals who might live there, their rights to live a normal and safe life, and the support they would get. I hope I was a real patient leader. The planning application was approved, much to the surprise of the officials present.

Be truthful

If you have to make cuts in expenditure, say so. Use meaningful language. Be open about the options that may be available and how these were devised. If timescales preclude real engagement, tell people without attaching blame.

If patients will have to travel further for part of a new pathway – say, elective inpatient care with community follow-up – be explicit about things like expected length of stay and the enhanced outcomes at a centre of excellence. Everyone will want better services but will equally want reassurance about visits from family and friends.

If you don't, there will always be someone who will find out the real reason and trust will be damaged. Trust arrives on foot but leaves on horseback.

The balance of power

'I've got all my experience of medical school and GP training behind me.'

'I've got 40 years' experience of living with this condition.'

Who is right? Why am I even asking this question? Although clinicians and society have changed, I believe that more can be done to enable patients to be real partners in their care.

Some patients may recall the days of their parents or grandparents talking about having to pay to see a doctor. Many will not question a doctor's decision. Healthcare workers are amongst the most trusted people in society. But we go to get your solution for something that's affecting *our* body or *our* mind, or both.

Others will become more informed about their health, using the internet to research, or learning from other patient groups. The fact that they do take time to find out more about their health is to be welcomed, but a clinician's response needs to be sensitive. We all know that there are many snake oil hawkers out there, but there are also reliable sources. Use your knowledge and communication skills to help the individual understand the strengths and weaknesses of each printout Dr Google has given them. Build on their anxious curiosity and the need to know. Form a real partnership.

Do you practice shared decision-making? Really? Are you offering patients all the information, and the space to reflect on it? Is there a poster about the Ask 3 Questions[1] approach above your desk? Speaking to lots of GPs, I know that the average 9 minutes is just too short and now I am asking you to give patients more time – or different time. Use the structures of shared decision-making as your joint agenda and see how it can change the dynamics in your professional relationships. With the move to total triage, are patients really involved in the decision about whether they see a clinician face-to-face?

Patient versus community versus population

Engagement can and needs to operate at a number of levels. Recall the language and experiences you've seen and heard today in your practice – what have your patients or their carers told you? Synthesise it, remember the themes, and then bring them into your next practice or network meeting.

Population health management is a more recent arrival identifying, for example, cohorts of people who make significant use of the NHS (mainly in secondary care). These statistics need to form part of a conversation with the patients they represent. We need to understand their contexts, their lived experience – triangulate the numbers and avoid designing new interventions without understanding individual's lives.

A local GP had a stack of vouchers for the local gym, but they were only valid at times which would not work for most patients. He knew his patients, so he hired a church hall and a sympathetic gym instructor, told his patients to wear whatever they were comfortable in, and off they went. People enjoyed it, lost weight, made new friends, and hopefully delayed the onset of diabetes. We ran through the statistics – attendances, weight loss, biomarkers, decreases in GP consultations. But this GP's greatest pride was showing a video of the 'class' in action and the personal stories of his patients.

I often wonder about the tension between the needs of the system and those of individual patients. Victor Montori speaks so powerfully about the dangers of industrialised care. The concept of trying to address unwarranted variation drew me on another part of my hike up Mount NHS. I learnt that we cannot, nor should we, eliminate all variation, because that ignores the fact that we are all different – standardise the hip prostheses you use, but remember you implant them into individuals, with different hopes and aspirations for their futures. When my prostate plays up, have a conversation with me about the evidence base and the NICE guidelines, but help translate them to me and my life.

Engagement doesn't just happen

It needs investment. A number of points come together here.

We need to give people the context in which we want them to be partners. People need to understand the situation about which we are seeking their ideas and contributions. They also need to understand any constraints which exist and why – how 'blue sky' can we be, or are there some heavy rain clouds which just won't budge?

We can begin our partnership with patients or residents before any formal events or meetings. Allow them to ask questions about any briefings; give them a jargon-buster. Just as a clinician's time is valuable, so is theirs. Asking them to suggest one thing to do better next time gives valuable insight into how effective we are being, as well as the humility to ask.

When thinking about the balance of power, there is also a need to invest in clinicians. They need to be prepared to leave their degree certificates and stethoscopes at the door, to use a different vocabulary, to be open to – and welcome – challenge. It also takes time and headspace to plan effectively, not to mention courage and resilience. We must not forget that clinicians are also patients. Imagine you were being referred to secondary care – what outcomes would you want?

Leaders need to think about how to create safe spaces. Patients and their carers may be anxious about their ongoing relationships with clinicians if they challenge. Clinicians in their turn may hear uncomfortable things about their practices.

Sometimes you need a ladder

It took more time to get to a place where we spoke to local patient organisations about any changes we might implement. Initially this was cursory at best, and we ticked the box.

When I was tasked with writing a service strategy for what we called multicentres – bases for primary, community, and voluntary services – I went completely off-piste. I invited patient representatives and potential occupants of the multicentre to a workshop. My aim was to agree on a vision of the concept and what it would actually mean to patients and their professionals. On arrival they found an artist's studio, with pens, glue, scissors, old newspapers, and flipcharts. Their task was to 'write' the front page of the local paper. Once they had done this, they sketched out the floor plans: imagine if someone with a long-term condition came in – how could we simplify their actual journey through the building?

By the time I was working as a delivery partner on the RightCare programme, the active involvement of patients was routine in redesigning pathways and challenging the established wisdom of so much that needed to happen in secondary care. Patients wanted to know more about how to self-manage and spot the signs of exacerbations in their conditions. They brought wisdom, born out of life experience.

I can see now how my hike fits with the concept of the Ladder of Engagement,[2] which ascends from informing others to collaborating and eventually devolving decision-making to them.

It is really important to take time over engagement. The learning that comes with each stage will strengthen you and give you courage and confidence to move up a level. Be aware of your surroundings – if your colleagues and partners are not quite ready to move on, don't rush it. There's more to lose than to gain. Celebrate success and learn from where things do not go as planned.

A letter to my younger self

Dear Owen,

When you joined the NHS, with all your youthful enthusiasm for helping society, it was the right choice.

At the end of the day, you and your loved ones are all patients or potential patients. What sort of care did you want for them? How did that question shape your work? How far did you walk in their shoes?

Presenting at that large public meeting was terrifying, wasn't it? You had to do it, but you learnt from it – you found Ethel and hopefully kept your body language in check. Your language changed for the good. You felt the fear and came through it. The learning was immense and valuable – as an NHS director, you apparently had power, but you've since learned to share it, haven't you?

The person specifications for some of the leadership roles you held called for the ability to manage complexity. There was no easy answer to engaging the local people you served, and you tried different approaches. People really appreciated the fact that you took time to talk seriously to them and involve them.

Others manage complexity more often than you do, so learn together. Remember that you're not alone in all this. There are organisations representing patients whom you can work with – community health councils, local Healthwatch, Diabetes UK, MIND, National Voices – share the expertise and don't duplicate.

You did OK, but we can always improve.

Owen

Commentary

'Oh, it's the system, you'll never change it'. We've heard that sentiment so often that it's hardly noteworthy. We know what it's like to feel like a cog in the machine, resigned to the thought that it was always like this and probably always will be. And yet there are leaders who dare to differ.

In Owen, we see someone steeped in the family values of service to the community, who is not only prepared to manage the system but to be a public face of it. We feel his discomfort as he discovers that the way he works with people, especially the public, doesn't 'work'. He wishes that the ground would swallow him up, which it doesn't, and he is left exposed. We also recognise his humility in being honest with himself about this, and his courage in daring to experiment and do things differently. Where he has been, we might do well to follow.

The system is the way we design and operate it. Owen shows that the system can be changed, one person at a time, through changing our attitudes and expectations of how we involve the people for whom the NHS exists: the patients.

Let's start by checking out how we feel about working with patients and involving them. What are the situations in which you currently do this? For example, it may be a patient participation group. What do you see as your role, and is it more about informing them or about involving them? What barriers to involving them further are you aware of? These may be your attitudes, the culture you work in, a skills gap, a lack of opportunity, and so forth.

Recognising where the resistance lies can get us off to a good start, but why would we want to involve patients more than we currently do? One perspective is to remind ourselves that complex problems such as we see in in the NHS can't be solved but can be improved through sharing the perspectives and ideas for change of those who are significantly affected by them. History is on our side, and in clinical practice we have progressed from excluding patients from decision-making to becoming more patient-centred in our attitudes. In establishing patients' needs and priorities, we are shifting our mindset from 'What's the matter with you?' to 'What matters to you?'

This attitude applies beyond the consulting room, where we need to involve patients because the system can't deliver a better experience if it doesn't reflect their values, experiences, and priorities. As Owen found, these can't be presumed or worked out from data alone. We need to hear the patient voice and to amplify it so that what patients think and feel is heard loudly and clearly.

We make changes to our service, hopefully improvements, all the time. How routinely do you consult patients not just to inform, but to seek their views and suggestions whilst you are forming your ideas? Why is that?

To help this voice grow, a new connection with patients needs to develop, building on patient participation to become a relationship, rather than a contract, of partnership.

What advantages do you see the partnership mindset bringing? And what are your concerns about sharing power and responsibility?

Partnership could mean that patients collaborate more actively on problem-solving and decision-making, and by being involved to a greater degree, they might also be expected to support joint decisions, which would help cooperation from the wider community.

Have you or your colleagues collaborated with patients on an issue or project that was important to you all? What was the experience like? What skills did you need, and were these developed through your training and education? If not, is this a blind spot that we should attend to?

Partnership can't be achieved without the mutual wish to do so, and as with team working, there are a number of requirements and skills that are needed to make partnership effective and rewarding. Let's briefly consider these.

The basic steps involve a greater degree of openness and the willingness to share important and at times, sensitive information in a psychologically safe environment. However, there are barriers to being more open, which we should be aware of.

When you communicate with other groups such as patients, how open do you feel you are allowed to be? Are you encouraged to openly share what you know, even if this would 'frighten the horses'?

Have you been advised to stay 'on message' and hold to a particular line, even when you didn't fully agree? More generally, how have you manipulated what you shared to get the outcome you wanted?

The information that is shared needs to be given in an understandable way not only about the service issue, its challenges, implications and proposals, but also about the ways in which lives are affected by it. Therefore, although it will include facts and figures it should also include the stories that describe how real people are affected. Owen describes how he learnt the importance of this and how he uses the mental image of 'Ethel' to keep him focused on what matters.

The service changes that are proposed don't just affect the people who use it, but those who deliver it. Therefore, the information and stories that need to be shared should reflect the experiences and concerns of these people too, not just the patients.

How do you feel about sharing the stories of clinicians, receptionists, and managers? Stories are emotive and can manipulate the group's interpretations and decisions just as much as statistics can. As a chairperson, how would you try to get a reasonable balance between sources of influence?

What we have described isn't just about sharing information; it's also about sharing vulnerability. This is important because it helps to build trust, which is the foundation of partnership. In practice, sharing vulnerability includes being appropriately open about doubts and mistakes and instead of appearing to have the best ideas, being able to ask for help. Our openness will invite the openness of others but with patients, reassurance may be needed. Even if they don't voice it, they need to know that there will be no repercussions of their care being compromised (or even favoured) by sharing their personal thoughts and attitudes.

If trust is the foundation of partnership, then helping people to be comfortable with conflict is the next layer. The goal here, with suitable facilitation, is to get everything on the table so that things can be recognised, debated, and weighed up. Look at it this way. If four of the ten of you are holding back on what you know, what you have seen, what you are worried about and so on, the group is missing 40% of what it needs to make the best decisions. That's not trivial, and one technique is not to finish the meeting until everyone has had a chance to say something that is significant to them.

There are parallels here with how teams form, and we should be prepared for a difficult storming phase when we try to share power, albeit with good intentions, but find that people are initially confrontational. This might occur, for example, if they are angry that they have been previously excluded.

Beyond working with patients in partnership, we are likely to find ourselves representing them in situations where they may not be there to speak for themselves.

What about when we are considering the health of a group, such as a diabetic community, rather than individuals; why is it so much more difficult to feel connected to such a group? What might help you to connect with your heart rather than just with your head, to feel compassion rather than just feel responsible? And why does that matter?

Owen, who represents patients nationally, describes how he seeks to understand what is important to patients and then use his leadership position to amplify their voices.

How might you do this?

We might for example use a range of narrative voices, having a range of 'Ethels' in mind. By using humanising stories on what matters to real people such as waiting times, continuity of care or days lost from work, we can complement the usual data sets on morbidity, mortality, costs, and so forth. Bringing together what matters to patients with what matters to the system keeps people on board and gives policy decisions greater credibility and, we hope, acceptability.

We have seen through Owen how the age of greater inclusion is upon us. We need patients' help much more than their compliance. They also need ours, so the points made above about greater engagement and collaboration and how to do this better are relevant to all those who need to work together.

We are co-dependent, and we may all be patients one day. When we interact in ways that reflect that belief, nothing is beyond us. As Owen shows, we can continue to endure a system that works against us, or we can reject being victims and develop one that works better for us all. The choice is ours to make.

Further reading from *The Leadership Hike*

Chapter 4 on using self-awareness to develop better connections with others.
Chapter 8 on the skills of communicating better.
Chapter 13 on how go from being a group to becoming a team.
Chapter 19 on persuading people and creating buy-in.

Podcast with the author

In this podcast, Owen Richards discusses:

- How the doctor–patient relationship is evolving.
- How patients are affected by changes in GP services.
- How to engage patients in their care.
- How to involve patients in shaping primary care.

Notes

1 https://aqua.nhs.uk/resources/shared-decision-making-ask-3-questions/
2 www.england.nhs.uk/get-involved/resources/ladder-of-engagement-2/

CHAPTER

14

Victor Montori

with Maggie Breslin and Dominique Allwood

Dr Victor Montori is an American endocrinologist, health services researcher, and care activist based at the Mayo clinic. His passion is to advance person-centred care for patients with diabetes and other chronic conditions. He is the author of the book Why We Revolt *and is leading a movement, a Patient Revolution, for Careful and Kind Care for all.*

On caring – taking a few steps forward for a patient revolution

The motivation – industrial healthcare

The pandemic of Covid brought into sharp contrast the challenges of the healthcare system, its sustainability, and its ability to care. Five years before the pandemic, however, we proposed that healthcare had corrupted its mission and had stopped caring. This evolution towards industrialised healthcare is set on processing patients with operational efficiency or, in the more modern parlance, with high value (i.e., achieving more with less). To gain efficiencies, however, industrial healthcare must minimise frictions, such as the difficulties in scheduling encounters between a particular patient and

DOI: 10.1201/ 9781003270492-15

a particular clinician, thus for example, disregarding their relationship or the continuity of their care, even when these are associated with better outcomes.

In this chapter, when we talk about care, we are characterising the actions of a person who notices that a patient (i.e., a person in need of care) requires attention, accompanying, fixing, or palliation. In approaching the patient, the clinician (anyone with the privilege of the bedside) will try to understand the patient's situation in high definition, in its biology and biography, in its sociology and psychology. When the clinician is familiar with the person, as when they have continuity in their relationship, this process of noticing what is new or different becomes easier and may happen in an instant.

After fully accounting for that situation, in agreement with the patient about its true nature, the clinician is then moved to respond. Responding to the problematic human situation of the patient requires taking action that is responsive to the problem and is consistent with the values, preferences, goals, priorities, and ultimately the best interest of the patient. To respond well therefore, clinicians must partner with the patient to co-create a plan of care that makes intellectual, emotional, and practical sense. This plan of care, built with competence and compassion, is the clinician's response to the problematic human situation of the patient. The evidence shows that this process of co-creation takes just as long as encounters without it.

Approaching the patient only with the intention to advance their situation, leads over time and with continuity of the relationship, to the emergence of a relationship between patient and clinician. The quality of this relationship often can only be described as adjacent to love, if not as love itself.

Within industrial healthcare, noticing and responding is made difficult by acceleration of the tempo of care, in visits that are busy, interrupted, and disrupted. As visits become bloated with mandatory tasks, the time to notice each patient and respond to each patient's agenda becomes effectively briefer even as total appointment duration increases. Without the ability to notice and respond, with the patient becoming nothing but a blurred image represented by a test result or by their description in the medical record, clinicians prescribe treatments for 'patients like this' rather than for 'this patient'. In people who experience multiple chronic conditions, these generic treatments accumulate in a poorly integrated and coordinated manner, placing a substantial burden on the patient. As patients attempt to implement all these disparate treatments and coordinate healthcare while negotiating rationing disguised as administrative barriers, they and their families become overwhelmed by the work of being a patient. Sometimes patients cannot implement the whole plan because it is too burdensome or because they and their caregivers lack the capacity to do so, or because that capacity is busy with pursuing the patient's hopes and dreams. When patients end up defaulting on some aspects of their care plan, healthcare's response is cruel. The patient, not their situation but their character, is labelled as 'noncompliant'. About 40% of patients with chronic conditions report that their plans of care are unsustainable.

Industrial healthcare is also cruel to clinicians. Clinicians go through their day unable to make a connection with the patient because they're spending a substantial proportion of their time in clinical encounters with a patient they do not get to know, completing mandatory tasks while clicking and completing fields within the electronic medical record. It has been estimated that clinicians spent 40% of the encounter time directing their attention at the computer screen. Unable to connect with the patient, they fail to gain from the renewable energy of care, an activity that, although exhausting, also replenishes and contributes to meaning and joy in the practice. Without these, clinicians experience burnout, as is the case for about 40% of them, and some exit clinical practice, reducing the access to and availability of care for patients and further burdening the remaining clinicians. Industrialisation renders healthcare unsustainable, to both the economies and the people that give and receive care.

Turning away from industrial healthcare

Efforts to change this situation through quality improvement, innovation, and research – like the ones in which the authors have been involved at their home institutions – abound. The new interventions, when designed to improve patient-centred care, often fail to normalise despite ongoing investments and the enrolment of clinical champions and supportive leadership. In contrast, administrative changes that promote efficiency and reduce costs tend to catch on without much effort. We propose that the 'soil' within which care-focused interventions are expected to thrive is in fact hostile to care. We set out to change this environment, to transform healthcare.

In 2015, we founded a charity called The Patient Revolution, Inc. The choice of describing this as a 'patient' revolution reflects our notion that healthcare professionals were not able to notice or respond to the increasing industrialisation of healthcare and the corruption in its mission. The task of turning away from industrial healthcare must then fall onto everyone, that is, on every person who would eventually become a patient in need of care. To work towards a healthcare system capable of care, we chose the word 'revolution' with trepidation. In a world that is marked by violence and death, so-called revolutions often start with good intentions and end up destroying the lives and livelihoods of those most vulnerable, people unable to escape or to use their resources to gain advantage. Revolutions are not generally desirable. And yet, the nature of the change needed in healthcare is so fundamental, so radical, that other words such as 'reform' or 'renewal' do not do justice to the magnitude of the change needed. The words 'revolt' and 'revolution' both refer to turning, and this indicates our orientation: to turn away from industrial healthcare and towards careful and kind care for all.

Careful care refers to evidence-based care that responds well to each person's problematic human situation, noticed in high definition, as part of a plan co-created with compassion and competence with each patient. The plan is formed within unhurried conversations, in which no time is wasted but the tempo of care is respected. These encounters are not only efficient (no waste) but also elegant (no haste). They result in plans of care that make intellectual, emotional, and practical sense to the patient. We also seek kind care, in which we see in each patient a reflection of one of us, of a next of kin. This is essential as it is hard to care for 'generic' others; the subject of our care must have a name. Their care should reflect how they would like to be treated, a platinum rule that invites curiosity and interest. Kind care is also a call for having deep respect for the time, energy, and attention available to each patient, as they would rather use these to pursue their lives and their loves than to complete healthcare tasks and medical errands. Thus, kind care advances patients' situations as it minimally disrupts their lives. Thus, a patient revolution would be required to turn away from industrial healthcare towards careful and kind care for all.

The action – change through research

This was not our first foray in trying to change healthcare. D.A. had been involved in leading numerous collaboratives and developing several networks focused on improving the quality and value of healthcare and advancing healthcare's role in the community as anchor organisations in the United Kingdom. M.B. has been a leader in design and service innovation in healthcare organisations, pioneering this work since 2003 at the SPARC Innovation Program and at The Centre for Innovation, both at Mayo Clinic (USA). V.M., a clinician and researcher, founded the Knowledge and Evaluation Research Unit in 2004 and has since been advancing evidence-based medicine, shared decision-making, and minimally disruptive medicine. Collectively, their work can only be described as successful insofar as it has advanced knowledge, patient care, and social determinants of health through quality improvement, innovation, and research within the existing system. What happens when that system's fundamentals are broken? One aspect of the work that the authors have taken on, which is pertinent for this book, is to recognise that while they can continue with their current activities, these activities by themselves are not going to achieve the kind of healthcare they envision for themselves, for their loved ones, for their communities, and for future generations.

The decision to pursue a patient revolution was not taken lightly as it requires taking on powerful organisations and avoiding misdirecting criticism to those at the frontlines of care. This was particularly hard at the time of the pandemic: clinicians at the coalface and other essential workers outside healthcare experienced the brunt of both the viral infection and the policies in response to the pandemic. We joined the population in cheering for them, as we hoped our commitment to transform healthcare resonated with the generous contribution that these essential care workers made to the well-being of their fellow humans. Our commitment to a patient revolution expresses our dissatisfaction with the insufficient power of the approaches that constitute our craft to change a system that is fundamentally inadequate, that has corrupted its mission and has stopped caring. It expresses our deep desire to bring care into healthcare.

Change through language – the pathologies of care

The first step in a patient revolution is to use language that stops hiding what is wrong with healthcare and is helpful to orient a different way of doing. You have encountered some of that language above: 'hurry', 'blur', 'cruelty', and 'burden'. We have described these as pathologies of care, a product of industrial healthcare adapting to the political, economic, and corporate determinants of healthcare and a manifestation of healthcare's focus on advancing operational and financial goals and reaching industrial targets. One key advantage of this language, in addition to its usefulness, is that it implies a way forward and away from industrial healthcare and towards careful and kind care. By focusing on its tempo, healthcare moves from hurry to elegance. By focusing on noticing without interruptions or disruptions, healthcare moves from seeing patients as a blur to seeing them in high definition. By focusing on responding with competence and compassion, healthcare moves from cruelty to responsiveness. By focusing on patient work, healthcare moves from being a burden to becoming minimally disruptive. By focusing on its culture, healthcare moves from the industrial processing of patients to caring for, about, and with patients.

Our focus on language doesn't stop at defining our method as a patient revolution, our objectives as careful and kind care, and our targets as pathologies of care. It is also important that in the words that leaders and clinicians use, we don't objectify patients, creating 'others' who are indistinguishable as individuals, but rather make every effort to see each one. This extends to health professionals as well. Take for instance the word 'provider', which describes both the care professional and the institution in which that professional works. This ambiguity makes the professional an indistinguishable and interchangeable part of the institution, while the term clinicians more clearly denotes anyone – therapists, pharmacists, nurses, physicians – with the privilege of being allowed to care at the patient's 'bedside'. Our focus on language manifests in our communications – websites, social media posts, and articles and presentations for professional and lay audiences – and in our 'manifesto', *Why We Revolt: A Patient Revolution for Careful and Kind Care*, first published in 2017.

Change through community – the Patient Revolution fellowship

It is not possible to understand healthcare from a single perspective. Thus, it was important to assemble a group of multidisciplinary colleagues who, passionate about transforming healthcare, arrived at that conviction through different set of experiences appreciated through the lenses of their diverse disciplines. Thus, a key step in our movement was to form an international group of Patient Revolution fellows who contribute to develop the vision of careful and kind care in practice. Fellows collaborate in an environment that reflects the environments of care we would like to see in healthcare. They are encouraged to notice and respond with competence and compassion, to bring their whole self to the work, sharing generously, and to be open, trusting, and ready to learn from and trust the other fellows. Each participant is encouraged to take initiative and responsibility, and together adapt methods and goals, a major challenge especially during crises like the Covid pandemic. The lessons learned in working with the fellows have shaped the notion that clinics that cultivate careful and kind care should be examples of so-called teal organisations in which people can be creative and realise themselves, work together to notice and respond to changing conditions, and be trusted to act autonomously and responsibly.

Change through action – the Patient Revolution clinics

In our journey towards a patient revolution, we recognised that a major stumbling block was the inability to imagine what we meant by careful and kind care, not in theory but in practice. Thus, the Patient Revolution fellows and governing board have been working to develop Patient Revolution clinics. These are clinical practices in which patients and clinicians, managers, leaders, payers, and policy makers, could directly observe and experience what careful and kind care entails in terms of the way professionals work with each other, the way they care for and about each other, and the way they care for, about, and with their patients and their communities.

To this end, the fellows have begun work on developing a playbook, thus moving from *why* to *how* we revolt. An extension of this work has been the identification of potential partners, existing healthcare organisations who may want to join the revolution and support the development of pilot clinics in which some or all elements of this playbook can manifest in practice. In the context of developing these sites, we expect to identify opportunities to advance the ways we care or how we support and enable care from the 'back office'. These opportunities make these demonstration or pilot clinics not only places of experimentation but also of innovation.

Another substantial stumbling block relates to our sense that a consensus about industrial healthcare's woes and about the need for radical change is emerging. Yet, it is not widespread enough such that people who are persuaded of this may feel alone and isolated. Furthermore, their conviction may falter in the face of healthcare's excellence in responding to trauma and other acute conditions or when seeing the results of wonderful surgical feats. We envision Patient Revolution clinics becoming gathering places in which people can connect, feel part of a larger movement, and join a community of learning and practice.

The next steps – a global network of careful and kind care

Starting from these centres of demonstration and community, we expect to see a global movement that will transform healthcare. The work of transforming healthcare is akin to that of building cathedrals. It is going to be hard work, the original blueprints may not guide the whole construction, every generation will leave its mark, and it will come to be much after the passing of those who envisioned it. Perhaps the global network will reflect this analogy, but the achievement of our ultimate mission, to achieve careful and kind care for all, may respond to a different analogy. That shared by Galeano, in which horizons stand for our utopian visions. When we walk towards the horizon, it walks away from us. And that, according to the artist, is the purpose of horizons, of utopias. To walk. Building these pilot clinics around the world and forming a global community are our initial steps towards the horizon. These actions construct the evidence we need to believe in a better tomorrow: a commitment to care, within and outside healthcare as a way of facing the threats to our humanity.

Leading with others, a movement for care is the easiest thing in the world. No one believes we are wrong in demanding that policies and actions get evaluated on the extent to which they represent the most caring response we can muster. No one argues about the importance of caring for each other, about each other, and for our environment. While there is no threat to 'what is' and little movement towards 'what should be' – despite the obvious voltage between them – without a clear practical path forward, there is no serious consideration, no forceful opposition. And then doubt arises: can a revolution, taken seriously, encounter no friction or resistance?

And so here we are. Years into it, with tens of care advocates taking early and simple action, harbingers of what is to come. In a world in which plans must be drawn for the next quarter, leaders of radical change must point at the next generation. In a world of attention deficits, leaders must tell stories that show to all what these early phases say about the future we could build if we persist. In a world of measures and hard outcomes, of money and reputation, leaders of care must point at the lack of fundamental humanity in our spreadsheets, prospectuses, and reports, and offer better models built on strength of numbers, on a solidarity without calculations. In a world of passive and inattentive consumers, leaders must awaken activism, foster focused action. In a world of isolation, leaders must weave communities of progress.

A movement of care requires careful and kind words, actions, and conversations. It requires knowing when to embrace the discipline of scientific execution and when to engage in the hard work of poetry. When to promote systems of efficiency, and when to create the conditions for care to emerge and evolve.

In negotiating these tensions, leaders will find darkness in the form of a question: 'What if we are wrong?' Seeking to inspire, leaders fear coming across as naïve, uninformed, disconnected from the harsh realities of scarcity and failure. Are we a joke? What if the naysayers are right? Their confidence fuels the leader's doubts. The leader blushes. But it is clear! Can't you all see it? No? The leader's hesitating silence is the provisional triumph of things as they are.

Doubt. Ridicule. Failure.

Try again.

Doubt. Ridicule. Failure.

Abandon?

Look up at the sky and find the lodestar. Point at it for the others to see. Tell stories of care, hear back stories of love. Tentatively whisper, 'onwards'. A roar bravely replies, 'onwards together!'

And so, the leader goes on.

Zoom out and you will see massive immovable slabs of cement, perfectly polished squares fitting tightly, forming the established pathway. In between those slabs, a bright green shoot.

Leadership as hope.

Commentary

More than anything else, Victor's impassioned voice is a cry from the heart. What makes it powerful is that it is not just a cry from *his* heart, but from the hearts of patients and caregivers alike; those whose purpose and meaning comes from caring about people as well as those people who need that care and with it, the understanding, support, and hope that it brings.

Although we nominally work in a 'healthcare' system, the growing reality is that although the data may show that health is being addressed, the feeling of care can be lacking and as a result, unhappiness reigns.

Does that resonate with you? Care, based on the interaction between humans who have a relationship, is under threat from the industrial process of implementing evidence-based medicine on a subservient population. How has that affected the care you give, both negatively and positively? What would you seek to retain from both approaches?

As with all complex problems, there may be no solution but there are better ways forward that require us to adopt helpful attitudes. For example, suppose industrial and relationship-based medicine or put another way, biomedical and biographical approaches, were each seen as having a legitimate place? The two lenses together can give us a high-definition picture of the patient, but as Victor describes, what we are fed and required to respond to comes dominantly from one perspective. Maybe as people who care greatly about health services, our task is to find a better balance. This could be one in which the power of data collection, algorithms, and targets is used to do what they do best, and sufficient time is allowed for the attention, support, and compassion that human interaction makes possible and requires.

To achieve this better balance, both approaches need to be respected so that they have adequate space. How would you describe what each has to offer to your team? We often feel pressure to focus on the biomedical because of performance and financial targets. How would you make space in a meeting for discussion of the biographical dimension, and why would you do this?

The 'noise' that we hear in the workplace is increasingly the clamouring of the biomedical machine, prompting us with data such as test results, gaps in data sets, and cajoling us with threats of missed targets.

How would you bring in the voices of the people, such as the issues, stories, and experiences of patients and team members? How would you use these to balance the noise of the data?

As leaders we understand the variety of ways in which people are motivated. Some may be interested in the human interactions; others may be more interested in the data. We need both, and that may be hard to remember if our own bias for one or the other is strong. Because leaders exert a disproportionate influence on the attitudes and behaviours of others, it may be important to check that we are not biasing our colleagues unhelpfully. This may happen if we inappropriately reward or censor people for the approach they take.

Suppose a colleague repeatedly failed to attend to data requests from the computer, deciding instead to focus on the patients' concerns. How would that be addressed in your organisation? Is that appropriate? How permissive is your organisation in allowing experts to deviate from biomedical 'guidelines' in response to what they have learned from the patient story?

The factors that we have touched on relate to the values of the team, which we may help to shape through our own attitudes and behaviour. For example, we may put competing priorities like human and data needs in context, so that they are both addressed enough. If our ultimate goal is to optimise health and well-being, we might highlight the importance of not overlooking what we regard as being important, but can't measure. As Einstein reminded us, 'Not everything that can be counted counts and not everything that counts can be counted'. The qualitative is as important as the quantitative, but it takes our leadership to change the culture so that these are more than mere words. For instance, we might be courageous enough to risk not meeting the measurable targets of performance because that time was needed for what mattered to the patient. However, as Victor points out, when the issue strikes at the heart of what gives healthcare meaning, purpose, and joy, then we have no choice but to go beyond the practice, get political, and do so collectively.

So, how will you speak out? And when?

Victor writes of an issue that has deep meaning for all of us and eloquently shows why we must address it. The reason that we have written this book is because we feel similarly about leadership. Our belief is that leadership is about doing what matters, not just what we are told to do. Every human being has that drive and most want to make life better in some way for the people they care about. This is the work of everyone, not just those elected or installed as leaders. The range of people and their inspiring stories in this book are proof of that.

Victor describes how the human world of caring and being cared about is being damaged by approaches that are dehumanising. Let us draw some parallels for the art of leadership from what he has to teach us.

Leadership is a similar 'human world' because it is all about the people, and it, too, has been damaged by approaches that don't connect well with them. Many of the requirements for humane patient care are the same as for effective leadership because both have the development of relationships at their heart. There is no shortcut to this. For patients or team members to respond to our influence, they have to feel understood and cared about. Unfortunately, caring about a generic group isn't a substitute for this; we need to know people personally enough and maintain a continuity of relationship that allows trust to grow.

And trust is important because it is at the root of how people cope with uncertainty both in clinical life when health is at stake and in leadership where motivation, effectiveness, and livelihoods are at risk.

What about how we get to know people and create a sense of direction? Noticing and responding to people's thoughts and behaviour is an ongoing process and can't happen if we are persistently distracted. We might be tempted to 'save time' by telling people what to do, maybe basing this on what the guidelines say or on the use of our authority, but this is not as time efficient or fulfilling as 'co-creation'. Also, if we fail to put the time in to develop relationships, we deprive ourselves of the opportunity to feel the renewable energy of caring. This energy can sustain us, but only if we take the steps to experience it.

No matter how well-meaning we are, we can easily be blind to the fact that if people are influenced by us, they can also become drained by us. Being a 'good follower', like being a good patient, involves effort. If we are aware of this, we can take steps as leaders not to overburden others.

These parallels are instructive and show how in many ways, leadership is an extension of clinical life, first helping individuals through sound relationships and then communities to be well.

Our passion, expressed through this book, is to help people understand and accept that they have what it takes to do what matters and to improve the world around them. All that is required is to care or, as Victor puts it, feel something 'adjacent to love'. If you have that, all else that is worthwhile will follow.

Further reading from *The Leadership Hike*

Chapter 3 on using our awareness of what's important.
Chapter 17 on developing a vision and sense of direction.
Chapter 25 on fostering our core values and being courageous for the long haul.

Index

D

E

F

G

H

I

J

K

L